Fresh Start

40 Day Marriage Bible Study

Aimee Larsen

Reprinted & Published 2018

www.homespunmom.com

Subject Headings: Marriage/Hope/Discipleship/God

Printed and Published in the United States of America

ISBN-13: 978-1721834624 (CreateSpace-Assigned)
ISBN-10: 1721834621
BISAC: Family & Relationships / Marriage & Long Term Relationships

Photography: Jaime Bewley Photography

FORWARD
by Ashley Shepherd

I will never forget meeting Aimee for the first time, her smile lit up the room and I knew I had to just walk up and give her a hug. It was an immediate divine appointment and I am so thankful for social media so we could stay connected. Our friendship grew but I knew God brought us together for a bigger purpose.

My husband and I married in 2005 with so many hopes and dreams but sometimes life can interrupt what you have had in your heart since you were a little girl. I dreamed a thousand times of being in the white dress with a long veil walking towards that handsome prince who promised to love and protect me forever. College was spent daydreaming of life with my husband: cooking new meals, hiking to mountaintops, and playing with our little ones—- all side-by-side. And for the first few years of our marriage some of my dreams of unconditional love came true. But with every bump in our plans, bill we couldn't pay, and dream failed came the stress that weighed our marriage down.

I started reading the Bible about marriage; grabbing every marriage book I could at Target, and praying A LOT. I sought out ways to try to change my husband and our circumstances and we experienced seasons of doubt on and off for 3 years straight.

We chose to fight for our marriage when the world was pointing arrows the different direction, then in May 2017 I got to spend uninterrupted time with Aimee and the Lord. I left that weekend with a vision for our life and 2 weeks later Aimee posted online about her 40-day marriage devotion. I knew it was for me.

By day 3, tears welled up and my heart started racing because I knew God was using Aimee's words to change me, not my husband. As His words penetrated my heart, I started to release our marriage into the hands of God, who had created it. Aimee's transparency, authentic heart, and genuine desire to help every woman see their marriage through the lens of God's Word, to value their marriage and their role in such a way that it honors His plan will shift your mindset and will fill your lungs full of hope.

Ladies, this isn't "just another marriage book," it's a Spirit filled, God inspired, and powerful way to encourage your heart to grow closer to the Lord. We weren't created to "fix" what is broken or lost; we were created to run into the arms of our Creator.

Ashley Shepherd
Founder and Author of "Beautifully Designed"

DEDICATION

To the Beloved of Christ, the dear precious women whom I have the privilege of speaking to, writing for, and praying over.

In Him is where you will find Love.
You are the object of His affection.

ACKNOWLEDGMENTS

My darling, James, thank you.
I'll love you forever.

IN THE BEGINNING

My husband and I started dating when we were 14 years old. Years passed, and we were married on a beautiful day in March and by May of the following year we were having our first baby and moving into our home that we had been building. Life happens, times get hard, and marriages struggle. It's a fact of life. No marriage is exempt from trials. We found ourselves no longer living the life we had dreamed and worked so hard to build.

Many nights I would lay in bed and cry of a broken heart because my marriage was not as I dreamed it should be. One day, I started talking to God about my hurt as I should have from the beginning. I was doing my normal every day chores. The tears flowed, the prayers spilled out, and with each confession I felt better. I was brought to my knees that day. So many private thoughts finally flowed out of me and straight to my Father who had been waiting all along. I wanted to know what I could do. I could no longer worry about my husband's shortcomings, I needed to grow as a Christian wife. The result, was this study.

I opened my Bible and secretly committed myself to 40 solid days of God directed studying. I recorded my study because I wanted to remember and share any revelation God gave. Day by day God revealed so much to me. He changed my heart, He fed my soul, and He healed a broken marriage. I began to pray over my husband, our children, and our home in ways I never had before. This dedicated time of studying changed everything for myself and many others as I have and continue to receive many private messages and emails from other women who have participated with me on my blog. They always say the same things, they were searching for something more and they found it with this study.

Please read this study with an open heart. Take from it only what God sees fit and I encourage you to pray before beginning. Here is my prayer for you…

Dear Lord Father, I pray with all my heart and with all my soul today that you reach down into the life of the reader of this study and bless her Lord as you have blessed me. Give her the wisdom she seeks to become a wife of purposeful prayer, an influence in her home, and a woman of gentle strength. Lord, we know that one cannot read your Word and not be filled. I pray that the hunger for a godly marriage and one that is fulfilling is satisfied. I pray that the thirst for your Word and wisdom is quenched. Father God, I humbly come to you today and ask that you open this woman's heart and mind to receive the sustenance of your Word. In Jesus name, Amen

Let's start fresh and refresh our marriage.

Aimee

WHAT TO EXPECT

The Head, Heart, and Hands

Yet this I call to mind and therefore I have hope: Because of the Lord's great love we are not consumed, for his compassions never fail. They are new every morning; great is your faithfulness. - Lamentations 3:21-23

The scripture above sets the entire tone of this study. It speaks of a fresh start every morning, a renewal that happens when we are faithful. This is a fresh start to your marriage and a fresh start to your day.

I have always been taught that there are three elements that make up a perfect approach to learning. First, we will start each devotion with a focus on *heaa* knowledge. I will use stories, scripture, questions, research, quotes, and more to appeal to your "intellectual buy in." We all know that the devil likes to use intellect to confuse our thinking because there are simply things that God knows and things we may never understand. Secondly, I will appeal to your *heart, your* "emotional buy in." We will reflect on what we believe, our values, our ethics, and the things that we love and want most. Thirdly, I will challenge your hands for a "behavioral effect". We will talk about what we will be doing differently and how to act in order to grow and learn from the scriptures we study each day.

Taking any one of these 3 pongs away will not build a stronger marriage, you very well will not move forward at all. You must study for knowledge and understanding, you must pray daily and give your heart over to learning and then you must take action. Keep your heart open to the learning process. I do not claim to be an expert, but what I do know is that when I opened my Bible daily God gave me direction and a plan. This is a very personal study for myself that I have felt led to share with you so that you too may experience God's blessings on your marriage. I encourage you to carve out half an hour or so a day that works for you and get started.

I don't want you to think your marriage has to be on the rocks in order to make it better. So, cast that aside. No marriage is perfect, there's always more room for God. Don't consider your situation better or worse than any others. The answers are all the same no matter the problems you face because our God is unchanging. I encourage you to journal daily and write down your thoughts.

DAY 1: PATIENCE IS LOVE

Be completely humble and gentle; be patient, bearing with one another in love. Ephesians 4:2 NIV

Take a moment to read it again. How does that scripture immediately make you feel?

Patience is, according to the Oxford University Press, the capacity to accept or tolerate delay, trouble, or suffering without getting upset or angry. Basically, those lacking in patience want things now and want their way. We naturally have desires and hopes that we want to see fulfilled immediately. Instant gratification almost doesn't seem fast enough at times. What this simply means is that there are times when we feel the world revolves around our own immediate needs. Being impatient has its drawbacks. People that are impatient tend to have more than enough feelings of frustration and anger. They can only seem to achieve short term goals; so, long term goals like a healthy marriage may seem far-fetched and they don't even know it. Let's compare the characteristics of an impatient person and a patient one.

Impatient Person

- Irritable
- Not very nice
- Unpleasant to be around
- Leaps before looking

Vs Patient Person

- Feels better about self
- Better able to accept setbacks
- Pleasant to be around
- Able to endure a time period of waiting.

My inability to have patience during a time period of waiting is why I believe God started this study with patience and He knew we would all want to see immediate results in our own marriage but there is a time period of waiting, a delay to develop.

As I was trying to come up with a clever story of having great patience with my husband…I drew a blank. Instead, I thought of a time when my husband was patient with me. Like the time he was sitting in the car on Sunday morning, kids dressed, hair combed, buckled in with their pop-tarts, while I was still trying to get ready. In my mind, I did him a huge favor and brought my make-up with me to put on during the drive (plus the natural lighting is fabulous of course). I have to say, I am pretty lucky to have such a patient husband who would make sure the kids are loaded in the car, fed, and listening to music while waiting on me instead of tapping his foot at the bottom of the steps and rushing me by telling me to hurry. For that, I am blessed. It doesn't happen every Sunday like this but for this lesson this is the day that was important.

I heard a sermon on television about patience and the one thing that struck me as something new was this… love IS patient. Now, every instance since, when I read the word "patient" in God's Word I insert the word "love" or "lovingly" or something to that effect in order to have a better understanding of what it means to be patient. It's amazing what happens. I give praise to our Lord every day for the patience He has with me and for His love. For God, they are one in the same and for us they should be also. Our God is patient and *long-suffering* with us. He can and will wait on us.

Rejoice in hope, be patient in tribulation, be constant in prayer. Romans 12:12

Insert the word "love" for the word "be patient" in the scripture above.

What does it mean to you to "love in or love your tribulation"?

It makes the scripture a little harder to swallow instead of sounding like an ideal way to live. When something is harder to swallow we put more effort into getting it down. What in the world does that mean to "love" our tribulations (hard times)? It is simple, your tribulations are what God is going to use as a testimony to others later. It might be hard to see it at the time, but you will find that when you share your testimony with others you grow to love your tribulations. Sharing your hard times with others gives them permission to share their hard times as well.

What are some tribulations you have had in your past? List them.

What are some tribulations you are currently under now? List them.

Do you believe that God will use every one of these for good?

He will. Read Isaiah 61:3

God's promise is to make the hard stuff, beautiful.

You get impatient with your own life, trying to master a habit or control a sin and in your frustration beginning to wonder where the power of God is. Be patient. God is using today's difficulties to strengthen you for tomorrow. His is equipping you. The God who makes things grow will help you bear fruit. ~ Max Lucado

With His strength, find patience. Be patient with yourself as you learn to be patient with your husband and show love.

Since God is so patient with each of us, we should strive to exhibit the same patience as well. Today, pray for your marriage and make it your challenge to show patience with your husband as well as yourself. Some of us (like myself) find it easy to throw around words of anger and frustration that can be hurtful. Others of us have our own personal weapons we throw when we are angry and frustrated due to lack of patience. What is your weapon of choice?

Today, I'd be willing to bet you will feel as though your patience is being tested. For today and the next 39 days, show patience and keep negative remarks and reactions silent. Remember, as you exhibit patience with your husband you should insert "love" as you remind yourself to be patient.

Love is patient, Love is kind. *1 Corinthians 13:4*

Now, study His Word on patience and talk to God about situations in your life in which you need His strength to help you endure with patience. Read: James 5:7-11

DAY 2: I DON'T WANT TO BE A SIDEKICK

The morning that I sat down to write this study my husband and I got the biggest laugh when we heard our littlest boy from down the hall yell, *"I don't want to be a sidekick!"* Obviously, there was an argument between two brothers and the youngest did not want to be Robin, he wanted to be Batman. In reality, any one of my boys could play the part of superhero. Not one is more special than the other, and all three hold a superpower that makes them look particularly adorable during their time of need (or want).

It is always challenging to describe the role of a wife without offending someone because it seems like everyone is offended these days, so let's stick with the Scripture here; God's plan and role for us is special. Think about it, no one wants to be considered the "sidekick" when they know they have equal but different powers. Right? Right! My "superpowers" as a wife and mother are different from my husbands "superpowers." However, we work as a team. In a way, I am his sidekick. Not because I am less of a person but because he needs me to be and I don't mind. Truly, I don't mind because I know that without my super powers by his side, he would be less than a man and no man want to be less. We are to make them greater. We are always supposed to use our powers (let's call them gifts), to lift up our husbands and make them better than they ever thought they could be. There is one gift we can all have as wives, kindness.

Kindness is one of the most powerful gifts we have. We use it by choice, just as we choose to be patient. We must sometimes learn to be kind. Kindness is always remembered by the receiver. In the shortest Psalm in the book of Psalms there is a verse that says this about kindness…

His merciful kindness is great towards us… Psalms 117:2

Just before this verse there is a great and powerful, universal call to worship because of His kindness. His kindness makes such an impact that a great request to thank Him and worship Him for it was sought out. It was the sole focus of the entire Psalm. Kindness.

How many times in your life have you heard "Love is patient, love is kind?"

Yesterday's focus was on patience. It was a day of learning to express love through patience. Patience and kindness are like two sides to a coin. It's been said that patience is used to withhold negativity, but kindness is used to bring a blessing. Kindness is used to make someone feel better or change their circumstances for better. It is not always innate and does not always come naturally but it is a superpower/gift any wife can have.

Be kind to one another, tender-hearted, forgiving each other just as God in Christ also has forgiven you. Ephesians 4:32

Who has recently shown you kindness in words or actions? How did it make you feel?

What kindness is God prompting you to show towards your husband? Will you obey?

A kindhearted woman gains respect… Proverbs 11:16

I led them with cords of human kindness, with ties of love; I lifted the burden from their neck and bent down to feed them. Hosea 11:4

But the fruit of the Spirit is love, joy, peace, patience, kindness, goodness, faithfulness, gentleness, and self-control. Galatians 5:22

Why kindness? God created you to be your husband's partner. I always think of the song by Blake Shelton; "God Gave Me You." I get all emotional and cry every time I think about what that truly means. God gave us to our husbands, as much as we'd like to think we chose them, we are a gift from God. God gives perfect gifts. We are gifts to them just as Eve was God's gift to Adam as a companion. Not a gift of ownership but one of belonging.

If God created the perfect wife for your husband, would you be her?

My answer is "YES!" Yours should be also, no matter your imperfections or his; God does not make mistakes. We make mistakes in how we handle situations, how we love, and by the attitudes we choose. God does not change His mind about His gifts. Being your husband's wife, helper, and lover is your divine calling.

Your challenge for today is to do something kind and unexpected today for your husband. You are to be a blessing while withholding negativity. Safeguard your husband from negativity, pray for Him today. It doesn't have to be a grand gesture, just something you know he will appreciate. Show kindness in a new and unexpected way and don't forget to be patient as well. -Proverbs 19:22

DAY 3: JOY IS A GOD THING

Whosoever finds a wife, finds a good thing, and obtains favor with the Lord. Proverbs 18:22

Looking at these words, I reflect on what this means for me as a wife and for my husband.

I am a good thing. Me! I am a good thing for my husband. You are a good thing. YOU! You are a good thing for your husband.

Your husband finds favor with the Lord because of YOU. Being thankful for the ways that your husband receives God's favor brings more favor. Thinking such thoughts towards your God and all that He has in store for you should bring you joy as well.

Can you recall a time when it seems that God has showed favor to your husband?

'Joy' is quite a complicated little word. This tiny little word can be found in the Bible more than 150 times. There are many different Greek and Hebrew words used in the Bible to convey joy. The one I want you to focus on is *makarios*. This Greek word means supremely blessed, fortunate, or well off. Go back to the question above one more time.

Images of joy that my mind brings are people leaping in the air and shouting as if their favorite team is winning. Wouldn't it be something if the favor the Lord has for our husbands caused us as wives to jump and shout for joy, wouldn't we have a permanent smile on our face to go with it? Let's discuss favor and what it is or just as importantly, what it isn't.

Favor is God's reward for obedience for choosing to simply walk the path that He has laid out for you. It is when God puts into play someone in your life to help you out with no strings attached. Favor is simply God's attitude of goodness and blessing towards you. It is not an exchange system. It is not a payment for something. Don't confuse it with the "you scratch my back and I'll scratch yours", kind of favor. It is simply that God looks down and sees your willingness to be obedient and has a desire to bless and help you. Such blessings bring a wife great joy when they are noticed. It is something to smile about, even rejoice over, so that others see you are grateful for the blessings that bring you joy.

We are given favor according to the assignment God has placed on our lives. When you married your husband, God saw that it was a good thing. God's favor then begins to move others to help us achieve our destiny and dreams.

A merry heart doeth good like a medicine. Proverbs 17:22

Years ago, in the fall I realized I was dealing with what some would call "seasonal" depression. I had never been depressed before, but I felt like I as in a not so sunny place. One day in my laundry room while the washer and dryer were busy swishing and humming I was unhappily folding tiny undies and way too many towels. I broke down. I was so unhappy. I wanted more in my life than this. I wanted more money for nicer things, to get my nails done, to actually pay a beautician, new furniture, carpet cleaned from all the kid stains, and a bigger car but most of all I wanted my husband to love me. Any ladies out there feeling me on this? I knew there was more to life than the never-ending story of laundry and God heard and cared about every single prayer and desire of my heart that I shared with Him. He cared even if to some those things were trivial. He cared more about the root of the prayer and what my heart truly desired.

May the God of hope fill you with all joy and peace believing, so that by the power of the Holy Spirit you may abound in hope. Romans 15:13

These things I have spoken to you, that my joy may be in you, and that your joy may be full. John 15:11

I know people that have far less than I do and are happy. They are happy and very content. They are thankful with what some would consider meager. During my little break down I realized that I was not just running low on joy, I was empty. How in the world does someone refill their life with joy? I mean really? Isn't there something we can do on our own to fill that joy tank? We can't refill our joy, but God can. I prayed for God to fill me with joy. With fists in the air I asked God to fill me up, but first He wanted to show me something. He needed to show me all the blessings He had given me. He wanted me to see He cared and actually does show me favor daily. It's my responsibility to recognize it. As always, my Gracious Heavenly Father was faithful and good.

God started revealing to me that I had so much to be appreciative of because my husband has favor with the Him and that transferred directly to our little family. Gratitude proceeded the joy. In finding my own joy through gratitude of His blessings and thanksgiving, I was able to spread that around to my husband and my children. I began to find it satisfying to fold tiny undies because my children had tiny undies. I found joy in folding towels because we were blessed with towels. I even enjoyed washing dishes because the bubbles were so beautiful. That may sound like I was taking it a bit too far, but was I really? I found the more I focused on the blessings, gave thanks for each one, the more joy I was filled with. It became the case that when I looked at my husband with joy in my heart, he extended the same favor to me. There is nothing more pleasing to a wife than to make her husband smile and laugh because he finds joy in her. It doesn't happen overnight, it doesn't appear after a single prayer. What does happen in the moment we begin asking for joy, change. Something changes in our very hearts. If we keep believing that we have nothing to be thankful for then we are telling the world that our God cannot do and will not do what we need of Him. He's our Daddy God. If we want joy in our lives, you better believe He's going to show you where your joy lies.

Joy must arise from a yielding to fulfill God's great creative purpose and seeing it accomplished. This is why we are born. Matt 25:21

I started compiling a list of blessings. I wrote down everything I was thankful for and the list grew. I wrote down ways in which I could see God showing my husband favor and myself as well. The longer my list became, the greater the joy I felt. This joy was passed on to my husband. We both began to smile at each other more. It was much quicker to point out the blessings for him and I found that most of the time, he was already aware of them before I was.

Your challenge today is to begin a list. I don't care where, how long, on what, or with what, create a list and thank God for the blessings, number your blessings, count as many as you can. I learned to do this a few years ago when I was reading *1000 Gifts* by Ann Voskamp. It's a perfectly beautiful practice to do throughout the day.

Romans 12:15

DAY 4: IN HIS IMAGE

I cannot love you as I love myself until I love God as I ought to love Him.
–Jack Hyles

When I first read this quote I immediately thought about how God made us in His image. He could have made us in any image, but He chose to make us like Him all the while letting us be ourselves. He doesn't twist or force our love for Him but because we were made from the very beginning to be like Him with a desire to know Him, so that we would seek Him, and He hopes that we will love Him. We are a reflection of Him when we grow in our relationship with Him. This is all one giant love story.

As I was mapping out this study I sometimes became frustrated with how messy my own thoughts became. This study was not mapped out and planned when I first started opening my Bible to seek Him and learn from His Word on how to become a better wife. So, to me it looks like a mess in hindsight and I struggled for years with even attempting to organize it. Then one day everything was wiped from my computer. Every new page I had written and polished and tried to transform into something beautiful from the mess that was written on my blog, was lost. I thought for a second that meant I should quit but God quickly reminded me through a random stranger, who sent me a timely email, who had read the study and thought it was worthy of my time and it was a work He needed me to do. I pulled an old hard copy that was rough and unpolished back out and wiped off my giant white board in my office and began mapping. What I found was that God had a plan all along. A friend once told me "if that study is impacting that many women while still very raw, imagine what He could do with it polished."

Let me back up a good 10 years or so…

When my babies were little, and I was a new mommy trying my best to raise those little guys, I had an overwhelming conviction about the "image" that I was portraying to them and others. I know I came across to others as unhappy, tired, and miserable, with nothing positive to say. Being a mommy to young ones is draining work and I was not being filled spiritually, my strength was weak. I was unchurched but had a heart for my Lord. Deep in my spirit I knew I wanted nothing more than for others to see God in me. I wanted to reflect our Father in all that I did. I wanted my husband, friends, children, and family to see something much different than what I was reflecting back to them. I knew that if nothing changed, nothing would change. I started praying because I didn't know how or what to change.

Then one day, I remember not too long after we had started attending church again, the pastor saying that the Lord was telling him something. At that moment it didn't matter to me what the Lord was saying, but that my pastor could HEAR Him. This seemed so foreign to me and it might seem supernatural to you too. I sat in my church pew with a new baby in my arms and thought, I want to hear Him too. My momma heart needed to hear Him, I prayed more privately and specifically that He provide a way to help me hear Him. My prayer also was that I wanted to reflect God and that I wanted to hear Him so that I could learn from Him. My prayer went something like this.

Lord, I want to be Your worker with a purpose in this life. I want to be a vessel for You to work from, a vessel you can fill so that You overflow out of me. I want people to see You when they look at me, but Lord I don't know how, and I desperately need to see, feel, and hear Your presence. Help me to know You.

Those words came from deep inside of me and over the years I have learned so much about being a vessel and the need to be continually refilled. At the time, I only knew it was a desire in my heart. It was a desire in my heart because it was His desire all along.

I praise you, for I am fearfully and wonderfully made. Wonderful are your works; my soul knows it very well. Psalms 139:14

So, God created man in His own image, in the image of God he created him; male and female he created them. Genesis 1:27

God created you for such an amazing purpose that He created you in His image. Let's think about the complexity of what God did. First, He created us. He knew that we would want to be close to Him, to be like Him and so, he did the simple favor with the slightest of a breath and created us in His image. Our God is a deliberate, thoughtful God. He does not make mistakes and He wanted more than anything for us to love Him because He loves us. Imagine how much harder it would have been for us to relate to God if we knew we were made unlike Him. If we were made unlike Him our thoughts might say…" Well, if He is so great then why didn't He do us the courtesy of making us like Him"; truth is, He did. He created both male and female in His image.

When you think of God's character, what words come to mind? Take a moment to write down a few to complete this sentence. God is…

I know I wrote words like protector, strong, unyielding, forgiving, wonderful, everlasting, loving kindness, and grace. The character of God does not change. God's hope is that we never reject Him, that we love Him and that we trust Him. He wants us to become righteous in Him.

In marriage, we want the same thing, don't we? We want to have a righteous marriage that reflects Him, that reflects the characteristics of God because God is good, and He is love. How do we do that? He doesn't leave us hanging or wondering. He wants us each to become closer to Him so that when a husband and wife come together, they are closer to Him.

Therefore, confess your sins to each other and pray for one another, that you may be healed. The prayer of a righteous person has great power as it is working. James 5:16

God wants us to be His reflection of love, not only to the world, but especially to our spouse. He has so much in store for us, if we'll only love and trust Him as little children do. As we turn our eyes and love towards God, His love is mirrored towards our husbands. We begin to see our husbands as God's children as well. God wants to give your husband the same love He wants to give you. Should you not be just as willing to give your love away as well? Don't you feel more alive, playful, impulsive, free, animated, frisky, and thrilled when you are loved fully? The list of how love makes us feel could go on and on. When we feel loved by God, we feel things like comfort, peace, satisfaction, thankfulness, and strength. Your list may be different than mine, but the feelings are universal; so should the feelings you express towards your husband.

We have only touched on the character of God. For today I simply want you to spend time in prayer and talk to Him about ways you can become more like Him. Listen for His voice today and watch for answers. He will speak to you and it can come in many forms. Ask for eyes to see and ears to hear and He will grant that for you. Ultimately, you are working on becoming a vessel for which He can pour out from you onto your husband. Which means you are more important that you'll ever know. Mirror the love that God has for us in your actions, a kind word or something particularly special that simply says "I love you."

If you abide in Me, and my words abide in you, ask whatever you wish, and it will be done for you. John 15:7

DAY 5: THE GREATEST OF THESE

Love. In Hebrew it is the word "ahab" and in Greek "agapé" but they both are action words for love. This means that there must be a conscious act towards the one you love. Biblically they mean something much deeper. Their meanings go beyond behavior and transfer into an attitude. Agapé love is described as a Christ-like love. One that is characterized as being selfless, loyal, unselfish, and with benevolent concern. It is the greatest of all and unwilling to yield.

The wisdom that is from above is first pure, then peaceable, gentle, willing to yield. - James 3:17

I was studying the parable of the Reed and the Oak, a story about compromise, and how the reed was willing to bend, while the oak was not. According to the parable, a giant oak tree and a thin reed were both planted by the river. Whenever a rain came, the deep roots of the oak kept firmly established, enabling it to withstand most winds. It boasted to the reed of its strength and made fun of the reed. It would, however, be blown over by a wind of sufficient strength. The reed, on the other hand, would bend to the right or left, even with a strong wind and never be uprooted. It silently waved from side to side. The conclusion of the story was that the oak, because of its refusal to compromise could end up losing its very life in the storm. The reed, though it would survive, could do so only by continually bending even during a storm.

Open your Bible to 1 Corinthians 13:4-8

I want to walk you through the characteristics of love so that you can see it reflects both feelings and loving acts.

- Patient and slow to anger (v.4)
- Kind and gentle to all (v. 4)
- Unselfish and giving (v. 5)

- Truthful and honest (v. 6)
- Hopeful and encouraging (v.7)
- Enduring, without end (v. 8)

Biblical love is not envious, proud, self-centered, rude, boastful, or provoking.

When I read this parable, my heart skipped a beat. God gave me a gift the day I read this and spoke to my heart about the love I should have towards my husband. At this very moment I can rattle of a list of things that my husband and I have disagreed on and some we will never will agree on. The list is not to terribly long, it's pretty short actually. On the top of the list is our dog, Hiccup. My husband never wanted a dog, I am a dog lover. My husband bends a great deal so that we may have this large, Boxer-Labrador mix, who sheds, is scared of storms, loves being in the house, but does not behave very well. I love that dense dog and he too makes me crazy, but I do realize that my husband truly bends like a wet reed for Hiccup and the problems that come with owning a dog. For me the joy of having a pet greatly outweigh the trouble he can cause. Like my husband, the reed was "willing" to bend, to give a little, even in a gentle breeze. In a storm however, it was steadfast, bending but not broken. If we start to consider our role in our marriage as a bending reed, our marriage would also be steadfast and unbroken. We all have areas in our marriage that we should be willing to bend a little for. Yes, we are all defensive in our nature and expect the same courtesies from our spouse, but we aren't studying on our husbands. We are studying on what God will have us do as wives, how willing we are to bend in our marriage. Open your Bible and let's explore together love as more than just a feeling.

1 John 3:11, 23; 4:11

Love is not optional, we are commanded to love one another. It breaks my heart to hear a friend say "But, I'm supposed to love my husband." All the while sobbing because she does not feel the love she expects to in a marriage. We all expect that heart pounding, fire in our bellies, head swimming love when we are married. I'm here to tell you that is not love. That is something else. There have been times even in my own marriage when I didn't "like" my husband. We can be disgusted by situations or behaviors but we, sisters, are commanded to love first. The rest must work itself out.

Desire for our husbands can wax and wane but love must be steady.

How does reading this make you feel?

Read: 1 John 3:14, 4:7, 20

Love is demonstrative. Our love for God is shown to the degree we show love to others.

Well, that stepped right on my toes. Ouch! Sure, it is possible to show love towards other people and not even know God but there is a different kind of love when we do know God. When we know Him in such a way that we truly love Him. Our attitudes towards those that hurt us, say mean things, ignore our feelings, and look for ways to belittle us becomes very much different than a worldly love. This goes beyond our feelings of hurt and bitterness and becomes a love that focuses on eternity.

Has there been times that you have deliberately withheld the demonstration of love? Why or why not? 1 John 3:17

Love is active and looking for a place to land. We are commanded to do acts of love. If we shut our eyes and ignore the needs of others, our love for God is called into question. When God put you and your husband together, He entrusted your husband to you and you to him. There are needs that arise and we are obligated to acknowledge those needs.

Is there a time when you must simply acknowledge the need but not act on it?

1 John 4:19

We are only able to love because we have been and are loved by God. This love causes us to respond lovingly towards others. If you are reading this study it is because you believe your marriage is worth saving, is worth fighting for, brand new, or just needs strengthening. Your role as a wife in this study is to open your heart to what God is trying to pour in. He loves you! His love is bigger and purer than you will ever experience on earth. You will find safety and security in His love, He loved you first.

As the Father has loved Me, I have also loved you. Remain in My love. If you keep my commands you will remain in My love, just as I have kept my Father's commands and remain in His love. I have spoken these things to you so that My joy may be in you and your joy may be complete. This is My command: Love one another as I have loved you. John 15:9-12

Reread (v9): A believer's continual connection to Christ is necessary for spiritual health and yields the fruit of love for others.

What do you expect from the people who love you?

What ways can you express love to your husband when he needs it?

How have you experienced the joy of loving others as Christ loves you?

How does your relationship with God impact your relationship with your husband?

3 ways that you can show your love today:

1. Give a small gift with a thank you note.
2. Reach out and revive your relationship with a fresh connection.
3. Make a sacrifice by thinking of something that may be putting a damper on your marriage, like TV, unnecessary expenses, time consuming hobbies, etc.; now get rid of it.

DAY 6: FAITHFULNESS

As Christian wives we are called to faithfulness, challenged to maintain a steadfast trust in God. Our faithfulness with Him is an ongoing relationship; and with Him, to the world, we are called to demonstrate a desire for a relationship with our Father. He remains dependable and committed, we do not. In the Garden of Eden our God placed the tree of knowledge. He created a situation where His children could choose whether or not to live by His perfect standards. Standards designed to protect His children and keep pure the relationship. The Lord gave mankind a beautiful gift in the dignity of choice. When it comes to our marriage we have a choice.

To stay faithful or not; to stay...*heirs together in the grace of life. 1 Peter 3:7* or to step into sin and into adultery. A theme that runs through Scripture is God's intent for husbands and wives to be faithful to each other. Fidelity in marriage is God's plan for His Kingdom and God's purpose for His children. Adultery is strictly prohibited. (Ex 20:14, Deut. 22:22) Jesus also condemned adultery (Mark 10:11, 12; Luke 16:18) and Paul denounced it as one of the "works of the flesh" (Gal 5:19). Basically, it's a big fat no, no.

Let me go ahead and say that I am putting "legalism" aside here. I will not go deep into the results of unfaithfulness because truly, I am no expert. What I want to focus on here is why we stay faithful to our spouses. No doubt that adultery is such a severe breach of trust and fidelity that it is noted as a permissible ground for divorce (Matt 5:32). If you have stepped into that sin, know you are forgiven when asked for forgiveness. If you are on the other side of that sin, it is time to forgive. If you have not stepped into that sin this is a lesson to help keep you faithful until the end. We cannot control our spouses as they too have been given the dignity of choices in this life, but we can control our own behaviors.

...heirs together in the grace of life." -1 Peter 3:7

I was reading a Facebook post recently from an old friend. She was divorced and had tried to have relationships since the divorce. One of the things she said that made me very sad for her was that she realized that she may no longer be able to grow old with someone. That every new relationship was starting from the beginning and she would not get to experience the fullness of what it is like to walk through a marriage from beginning to the full end. Her statement made my heart ache for her. I understood exactly what she was saying. It was more about experiencing all the seasons that God intends with a lifelong marriage. I have no doubt that she will find someone to love her until the end and that God does have someone waiting for her if she'll trust Him, and she can still experience that fullness.

I have friends that have walked through the storm of adultery, some of those marriages were healed and some were destroyed. I have friends that are walking through it now and some that are in the midst of the sin itself and it has not yet been revealed. Infidelity is everywhere. It is hidden in the dark places but where there is dark there will be light.

Jesus taught that adultery begins in the heart (Matt 5:7, 28, 19:18, 19) and is rooted in lust. Many a marriage has suffered greatly because of "emotional adultery" which Jesus taught was just as serious as sexual immorality, and our minds struggle with this. You may be reading this and imagining that my marriage has not experienced any of this, that I sit on a pedestal and preach with a finger pointed. That is not the case and I am ashamed to say there was a time when I myself was the guilty party.

When I first wrote this study I was also seeking God's guidance on the subject of faithfulness. I was struggling and only I knew it. A deeply emotional betrayal of the heart was happening. My emotions were all in the way. I was in the midst of a storm in my marriage that felt like it had an uphill climb and I was looking for a way out of my misery. I thought I was finding it in another relationship. It seemed innocent at first, but that line seems very blurry and it seems that there is all this grey area, but really, there is not. In my heart, I was cheating on my husband and I regret to think that if given the opportunity it would have become more. I praise God today for taking that desire away of seeking something different for my life and turning my eyes back to the one man who chose me.

I realize now that it is my choice, it is in my control as to whether or not my husband and I are "heirs" of the wonderful things this life has to offer, or I can "error" and ruin it all. Husbands have their own choices to make but we as wives have ours. We have the power to decide if we want to be happy because happiness doesn't lie within our husbands or within ourselves, it lies within Christ. For the sake of my marriage and our happiness I want to grow old with my husband and be "heirs in the grace of life." I had to confess to my husband my heart, it was the hardest thing I have ever done but he understood because he also knew that our marriage was rocky. That was the first step, looking the sin in the face, asking for and receiving forgiveness. I will forever love my husband for the grace he showed towards me. I may never truly know how his heart felt. His forgiveness left me at his mercy and in a vulnerable place that changed the dynamics of our relationship but strengthened our marriage.

You too can have the bounty of goodness that God wants you to have. Whew, didn't that sound a little preachy…. bounty of goodness, but it's true. God wants us to be happy and love each other. He wants us to be partners in the goodness of life that He has to offer. We are our husband's helpers by design, their friends, a gift to them from the one we call Father who is gracious and good. We don't need to spoil it no matter our circumstances. God made us to be our husband's helper; made to meet their needs here on earth with His help. God will meet their spiritual needs. We are our husband's companions and we are there for good conversations, for uplifting, for support, for encouragement, and so much more than we give ourselves credit for. Remember, they need us! No matter how hard our marriage becomes God intends for us to live life with faithfulness, thanksgiving, and joy. I have had a much deeper appreciation for my purpose as a wife.

Today, if you have experienced either side of infidelity in your marriage, whether it is from your own doing or your husbands I need you to know that God is the ultimate healer. If it was emotional or physical, it doesn't matter. I encourage you to seek God's strength and wisdom on this topic. Remember that God does not make a mistake, we do. I pray a hedge of protection around your marriage and encourage you to do the same.

Read: John 8:3-11 & Ephesians 5

God promises to make the value of trouble a door of hope. Jill Briscoe

DAY 7: SELF-CONTROL

As you may have already come to know, I love to talk out loud to God and we work together on my daily tasks. As I fold clothes or load the dishwasher, He is there with me as I serve my family and He listens when my heart is heavy, and He loves it when I am giving Him praise because I saw the little things that He did for me. I was caught off guard one evening because it was His speaking that opened my eyes. As I was asking for guidance and help He spoke to my spirit… *My sweet child, I cannot control your actions. You are in control of more than you realize, everything you do matters. I gave you free will and the knowledge to make decisions. I expect you to come to me for help, but it is your responsibility to act in such a way as to honor Me.*

It that moment He felt so near to me that I realized that He makes up every fiber of my being. That is why He felt so close. He knows our hearts, our minds, and every hair of head on our head. See Matthew 10:30. He made us the instant we were conceived but thought of us long before then. He knows us in and out. (Read Psalm 139:13, Ephesians 1:4) He is more mysterious than anything we can imagine. He is in control of every function of our body, He commands our hearts to beat and breathed life into our lungs. He works at the smallest molecular levels and still remains our God. There comes a point in our make-up that God let's go and gives us control. I like to think of all the images I've ever seen of a daddy helping a child learn to ride a bike. He eventually let's go, to experience the fullness of life while staying right with us and never tiring out of picking us up, giving us encouragement, and helping us try this life, daily, over and over again. We may never quite "master" this life, but He sure lets us experience it. He can step in at any second and change our direction or say, "rides over" time to go home. Ultimately, He loves us deeper than we can image and wants the best for us.

God spoke to me through His Word on my self-control, or lack of. He gave me direction to help guide me when I am coasting through life and making choices. He also reminded me and wanted me to remind you that in all times He is there to speak to you when you need Him.

At the time I was preparing for this lesson for myself, my marriage was painfully unhappy. Self-control was the point at which I tend to lose my footing, stumble, and fall. It's where the deepest wounds happen, and they take a great deal of time to heal. Those wounds are not only mine, but they become my husbands as well. My lack of self-control is why my husband expected nothing greater of me. It was predictable, and my temper got the best of me. If he wanted to push a button to make me angry, he easily could. So, when God spoke directly to me on this topic He was addressing my weakest part.

As Christian wives we must consistently work on ourselves. It is essential to our personal development, spiritual growth and Christian service that we study on, practice and learn how to exhibit self-control. It is not a natural behavior of anyone to have self-control as we are all born selfish and it is received as the crowning fruit of the Spirit. Read Galatians 5:22. Sometimes, when I feel lacking in a fruit my prayers become banging on heavens gates cries to the Holy Spirit to give me what I need. He will not withhold it.

What are the Fruits of the Spirit?

There are 9 and are you sensing a theme yet in what we are studying?

Sisters, this is where we dig. This is where we pray. As followers of Christ not only are we to receive the blessings of God but also be a reflection of His character to all whom the blessings encounter. Godly virtues are the fruit of the Holy Spirit and are evidence of our salvation, the genuine work of the Holy Spirit.

"We can do no great things, only small things with great love." *Mother Teresa*

Matthew 26:6-13 Is a story of extravagant love. Mary did something over the top, she didn't care what anyone thought and stepped across culture norms to show her Savior how much she loved him. We truly have no idea what she was thinking but what she did was deliberate. She poured out her expensive perfume onto Jesus. Her act echoed the preparation of a body for burial. She knew He was going to give it all for her, for us. From her precious alabaster jar, she anointed Jesus with her love. When was the last time you were deliberate with honoring your husband? No matter what the world says, what is considered norm, it's time that women rise up and acknowledge our precious place alongside our husbands. Only you know what would honor your husband. Consider today of being deliberate and self-controlled in how you honor him. Mary broke open her jar and poured out a love offering. What could be your love offering? Pour it out. I promise, what you pour out to honor your husband, God will refill. Are you willing to pour out your time? Money? Gifts? Talents? I pray your extravagant offering of love is received with great joy.

DAY 8: OH GOODNESS

Being confident in this, that he who began a good work in you will carry it on to completion until the day of Christ Jesus. Philippians 1:6

Sometime ago I had written on a slip of paper "Philippians 1:3-6 & 8-18". Just below that I wrote, "blog, share about husband." I had written on that slip long before this devotion was even thought of. Actually, I found it in my Bible as I was getting ready to do this devotion. It had been written and forgotten. I honestly can't even tell you what my initial reason was for writing the verse down, but I knew it would be important. Read Philippians 1:3-6

When I read these opening lines that Paul wrote to the people of Philippi I pause at verse 5. Here Paul is acknowledging their financial support. At this time, he only alluded to receiving the gift; later he would thank them specifically (Phill4:10-19). Paul was in prison when this letter was written and what little goodness he as experiencing he was certainly thankful for.

Let's read Philippians 1:6, again.

What is Paul confident about?

Do you believe that God has created a good work in you? Do you believe that He is doing a good work in your marriage? Do you believe that He will see it to a flourishing end?

Paul also outlines many things we should be doing and considering as we work on our marriage.

1. Thank God for His goodness every time you remember Him.
2. Pray to God with joy.
3. Know the works that He is overseeing in your marriage will be good until the day of Christ.
4. Our love will grow with knowledge and experience.

So, what is goodness?

Goodness is the result of love, joy, peace, patience, and kindness at work. (Gal 5:22,23) It is the outward expression of the inner change of our believer's hearts.

Read 2 Thessalonians 1:11,12

God counts our marriage worthy of its very calling, to glorify our Lord Jesus Christ.

There is nothing sweeter to me than hearing a child talk to Jesus like He is a friend. I know my favorite is listening to my babies pray. They love Jesus. At the dinner table they tell him so and at night they lay in bed and have conversations with Him. Wouldn't it be nice to be more like little children? They are so humble and pure. I love to hear them thank God out loud for whatever they can immediately think of or what has been on their hearts and sometimes just whatever is in sight distance. They are comfortable in the role of the one giving thanks to God for all His goodness.

A friend and I were talking about our husbands and how they were not comfortable praying out loud in front of people. They are intimidated by others who are good at speaking "Christianese" when praying in front of others. You know the ones; their voice rises and falls to stress the importance of the important words. Some people just have that dialect and tone that makes their prayers seem…professional. I have prayed for my husband on this matter for years and to be honest, myself as well. I want us to be comfortable praying in public, in front of strangers, and even in front of our own family and not feel we have to pray any certain way. We don't have to speak "Christianese", while it's awesome to hear, God just wants to hear that our hearts are thankful for His goodness.

I was raised in church and went each time the doors opened. My husband, when we met in middle school, did not know if he even believed in God. While we were dating in high school, he was saved. He fell in love with Jesus too. Over the years I have watched his faith grow to become so enormous no one could ever deny it. This past spring, I had a sweet lady speak to me on my husband, she had never met him. She touched my wedding ring, thanked God for my husband and proclaimed that he was a great man of God. The touching of my ring, the prayer, the woman whom I'd never met before, none of that took me by surprise. However, saying "he is a great man of God" made me take a deep breath and become very still. I soaked in the words. Her words forever changed how I viewed my husband.

I have been praying for my husband for years to desire to read his Bible more, to pray more confidently at the dinner table, to minister to our children, to find joy and purpose in tithing, to become the spiritual head of our home. All the while God was hearing my prayers, He was building my husband and I never saw it for its worth until the words of a stranger peeled the scales off my eyes. I drove home with those words ringing in my ears that day. She proclaimed that my husband was the man I had prayed for. God is so good. He is waiting to do the same for you, sister. Whatever flaw you see in your husbands, God acknowledges. He may not agree but if you pray for your husband to become a great man of God, do you think our loving Father will deny the request? He most certainly will not.

One of my favorite memories of my husband and children will always be watching him kneel beside my boy's bed and read them their Bible story and devotion. He was like a child himself; never having heard most of the stories in their little books. He read them in awe and grew in knowledge of God's Word along with our boys. It was quite something to witness. It takes time ladies. My husband is still growing into the man our Father intended him to become just as I continue to grow as well. His goodness is what nurtures that growth.

Take a moment to think about recent conversations you have had with others around you. Have you felt nourished by encouraging words? How did those words lift you up? How did you respond?

Think about a time when someone's language wounded your spirit. Maybe you were shocked by a thoughtless comment from a neighbor or struck down by a destructive argument with a family member or friend.

Words are powerful when we speak them to each other. How can we show others God's goodness with our words? Where do we draw that goodness from? Can we extend that goodness to our husbands?

We all know what foolish talk and cruel words can do and how they wither our very spirit. Just as even foolish words can bring death, words have the power to bring life. Truth, when spoken with love, joy, peace, patience, and kindness can lift up a discouraged soul, restore dignity to the oppressed and heal broken hearts. God places great importance on our words. Paul also said *Let your conversation be always full of grace, seasoned with salt, so that you may know how to answer everyone. Colossians 4:6*

Your words have the power to breathe life into your marriage or put a nail in its coffin. You can wound your husband's spirit or protect your husband's dignity. Choose your words wisely.

Let's do something to help inspire us. Let's make a list. Grab your journal, a sheet of paper, the back of a napkin or right here in your book and write some words that you like to hear, words that encourage you, words that are full of goodness. Let's challenge ourselves to use the words like these today to lift up our husbands. Speak the words into your husband. Pray these words over your husband. Let's God's truth and plan for your marriage begin to take root and flourish.

DAY 9: WITH PEACE

I love reading my Bible and spending time in prayer. When I have time to sit and not worry about what the kids are doing or what chores need to be done, I just read and pray. God reveals so many things when I spend time with Him. His Word becomes so personal to me and He will do the same thing for you. When do we find time to read and pray? Some of us have to carve out time, maybe in the fringe hours of the morning before the house wakes up, maybe while the kids are all at school, maybe after everyone has gone to bed or even during your lunch hour. We all crave a time of peace.

Catherine Marshall once said, "*The purpose of all prayer is to find God's Will and to make that Will our prayer.*" In those moments when we find God's Will, we find peace.

Peace has so many meanings such as rest, security, ease, quiet, to keep silent. Peace is used many times in the Bible and in the original Hebrew word, *shalom,* it means peace as it is found with Him, to be with Him, perfect peace, and completeness.

Take a look at Romans 5: 1,2

Therefore, having been justified by faith, we have peace with God through our Lord Jesus Christ, through whom also we have access by faith into this grace in which we stand, and rejoice in the hope of the glory of God.

The hinge word is *peace.* Underline it in your Bible.

Peace = with Him, such as to be at, perfect peace, completeness.

Peace is a gift from God.

The Lord gives strength to his people; the Lord blesses his people with peace. Psalm 29:11

In both Old and New Testaments, peace is described as the result of having a right relationship with God and with others. The Greek word *eirēnē* has the meaning similar to the Hebrew word *shalom.* A sense of well-being and fulfillment is the spiritual, peace that comes from God and alone is dependent on His presence (Gal 5:22)

Spiritual peace is experienced during times of trouble and turmoil by believers who walk in the Spirit despite everything going on around them. This is the promise of God (Ps 29:11). Watching the news every evening is enough to cause even the godliest, most optimistic woman to want to stay in bed and pull the covers over her head. It's scary out there girls and a girl named Abigail knew that it was.

In 1 Samuel 25: 1-42 we find a story about Abigail. Abigail was a very intelligent and beautiful wife but married to a wealthy scoundrel named Nabal who was harsh and overbearing. Some women today are in unhappy marriages by their own choice, but Abigail probably entered this union by no choice of her own because arranged marriages were most common. This woman of faith acted humbly and wisely by giving David and his men food to save the lives of the household.

Read 1 Samuel 25:1-42

Nabal did not appreciate what David had already done to protect his fortune. When David's men asked for help and were denied David wanted revenge, but God sent a woman, Abigail, through the wilderness with sustenance and appreciation. She admitted that her husband had made a mistake and should not have turned away David's men but that she was sorry she did not greet them first. David spared their lives and thanked Abigail for obeying the Lord by seeking them out and providing what they needed. Most importantly he thanked her for stopping him from murder.

Abigail offered hospitality in the face of hostility, she was an *intercessor* for God. Ultimately, Nabal died of "natural" causes. When David learned of his death, he pursued Abigail as his wife, the intercessor.

Intercessor is one who is in such vital contact with God and with his fellowmen that he is like a live wire closing the gaps between the saving power of God and the sinful men who have been cut off from that power. ~Hannah Hurnard

I want to focus on the word intercessor. This isn't a new word to me but recently, I realized that was what I had become for my husband and family. There is another intercessor in the Bible, Anna. She spent her days as a widow in the Lord's house honoring Him, praying for others, and serving as a prophetess by speaking God's truths. She loved the Lord with all her heart. When she found herself alone at a presumably young age, she turned straight to the Lord. She spoke to many people about the coming of the Messiah with such hope and belief. Her story is a brief but amazing one. Abigail and Anna both served others by interceding for them.

Ladies, we are being called in this day and age to not only pray for our husbands but to intercede for them in prayer. In doing so, we become peacemakers. We are called to kneel in prayer, bang on heavens gates with our voices, enter the throne room of God for our husbands. Isaiah 62:6-7 says ...*I have appointed watchmen; All day and all night they will never keep silent. You who remain the Lord, take no rest for yourselves; and give Him no rest..."* You my friend, are a watchman for your husband. The power that you have as an intercessor will astound you. Standing guard over your husbands promises from God with prayer and thanksgiving moves mountains in your marriage. He brings direct peace to your heart. Your prayers are heard; the Lord hears your cries for your marriage and your husband.

Ephesians 6:18 tells us *with all prayer and petition pray at all times in the Spirt, and with this in view, be on the alert with all perseverance and petition for all the saints..."*

Do you hear your calling? Do you see your importance and purpose in your marriage? Does your heart beat faster knowing that you have the power within you to intercede for your husband? Imagine! Dream! Take hold of the vision that God is putting in your heart for the marriage you so desire. Pray. Petition.

The good news, when you're tired, weary, wordless, lost, confused, and feel the fight is gone. The Holy Spirit will intercede for you. (Romans 8:26 & 27) I cannot press firmly enough that you need to open God's Word and read this for yourself. Be blown away by the power you have in your prayer.

While we may not currently have an army camping out in the woods behind our houses or war going on in our community, we may have a war going on right in our home. There is a spiritual battle going on out there to take what God has made good in your marriage and destroy it. Hostility and words as weapons can bring a great deal of damage to a marriage. When you become aware that your home is no longer at peace and that the crisis is escalating it is time to ask God to give you discernment to think quickly and act decisively to stop the attacks on your marriage, attacks are sometimes subtle, but you feel them.

You have the power to intervene with lovingkindness on your lips and grace in your heart. Concern yourself with all that you have to offer and use the resources God has placed for you to use. Like Abigail, seek God to help find a peaceful resolution to a possible explosive situation.

Can you think of a time when your husband could have used your peaceful intervention?

What about right now?

DAY 10: GENTLENESS

At the moment I am writing this, my thoughts are swirling in my head about this topic and the distractions are…distracting me. It's a lazy Sunday afternoon and while I sit and try to sort out my thoughts my husband and boys are outside my window tossing a football around. I have a stack of note cards with information I have studied on "gentleness", but all the knowledge in the world on the topic doesn't teach you a thing until you experience it. As I'm typing this my baby boy comes in says "Hi Momma.", hugs me and leaves to go back out. That was all it took.

When I think of gentleness I think of a new mother touching her newborn baby's cheek for the first time. I think of a stranger offering food to the homeless on the street in such a subtle way that it goes unnoticed by the crowds. I think of a nurse who leans in to an elderly patient and speaks loving words of strength. I think of a daddy softly reading a Bible story to his children after tucking them in at night.

Until the day I die I will be learning how to love my husband because my love is so imperfect and I'm sure you feel exactly the same. God's gentleness in leading us through this study so that we could learn how to love and keeping us humble so that we can bear to do His Will here. Your marriage has been prayed for, I pray a unity of the Spirit within your marriage and declare within it, the bond of peace in the powerful name of Jesus.

Philippians 4:5 says "*Let your gentleness be evident to all. The Lord is near.*"

Oh, how the scriptures adore gentleness. Especially during disputes. Paul was working so hard to create unity among Christ followers and how was he supposed to do that? With rejoicing in what they had in common, the Risen Savior, and with gentleness. Paul wanted the focus to be on their common joy and not on their differences.

As a husband and wife, we are different. We are two completely unique individuals with ideas and beliefs that came together in union. Our differences can easily divide us, if we focus on them. When beginning this journey of a study with the Lord, He pressed into me that this study would not be about our husbands. We were to only focus on how we could become better wives. No longer are you focusing on how to make your husband fit a mold you have designed, you are now praying for and working on a marriage that fits God's mold and design.

Let your gentleness be evident to all. Reading that, do your thoughts carry to a time when you may have had a conversation with a friend about how angry you were with your husband and what you intended to do about it? Did you ever hop on social media and tell the world how lazy or unreasonable your husband has been? Do you ever feel the need to shout out how upset you are with him? Is that letting your gentleness be evident to all? My toes are sore every time I open my social media memories and it shows me what I made evident to all before this study. I get to travel back years and see when my babies where little and grieve for that time again and relive for a moment the things that were most important to me, but I am also reminded of how miserable I was in my marriage and how evident it was.

Gentleness diffuses anger and hostility. We are called to focus on things that are true, noble, right, pure, excellent and praise worthy. Things that are beautiful, positive, and pure. (Philippians 4:8) The easiest way to transport your thoughts to these things is by way of thankfulness and gratitude. When you begin to appreciate all the small gifts, the tiny beautiful things God has laid before you then spirit of gratitude brings nothing but peace. Speaking words of encouragement to your husband, being content with the gifts God gives, will draw him closer, even when you are hurt, in a crisis, or in pain. When your gentleness is evident to your husband, he will know the Lord is near.

The quality of the heart is counted as being more influential than outward beauty in wining an unbelieving husband to Christ. (1 Peter 3:1-4).

The gentleness of a woman towards her husband is precious to God. I am not always gentle nor have a heart of gold. A lesson I am always learning is that God is perfect, I am not. I am not, they are not, and this world is not but He is!

Throughout the years I have found that any unhappiness in my marriage truly came from having unrealistic expectations and being ungrateful. My expectations were the source of much of my own doubt and misery. I have this dreamy idea in my head that when my husband is home that we are like kids again, we are laughing, loving, and listening.

The reality is, life is hard, and marriage takes work. One fall weekend, we had to two boys that had to be at two rainy football games in two different cities at two different times. We had to part ways. We came home like cold, drowned rats and sat on 2 different couches. I cooked dinner while he sat with an ice pack for his back that's been bothering him and all the while I tried every way from Sunday to get him in the kitchen with me. By bedtime I was resentful he never left the couch except to come to the dinner table and then when bedtime came had his own "expectations" if you catch my drift. I pulled the covers up over me, laid facing the edge of the bed, and tried to pretend to be asleep. It didn't work. In the end, I told him what was bothering me, and he said, "Let me go ahead and tell you that tomorrow may not be much different; so, go ahead and lower your expectations. That way you won't be so disappointed." Ouch! He was right. He wasn't gentle about it, but he was right. My expectations were unrealistic, as dreamy as they are, they just aren't realistic in my house. The huge disappointing reality was that when we put our own unrealistic expectations on our spouse it can get pretty overwhelming. We have to remember that our husbands are not perfect, but that our God is. Having a gentle spirit towards our spouses could resolve many of those expectations.

I will proclaim the name of the Lord. Oh, praise the greatness of our God! He is the Rock, his works are perfect, and all his ways are just. A faithful God who does no wrong, upright and just is he. - Deuteronomy 32:3-4

Soak that in and then read the next two versions.

As for God, his way is perfect; the word of the Lord is flawless. He is a shield for all who take refuge in him. - Psalm 18:30

The law of the Lord is perfect, reviving the soul. The statues of the Lord are trustworthy, making wise the simple. - Psalm 19:7

No one is perfect, only God is. I have really got to give my husband a break. How about you?

Have you expected your husband to live up to your expectations? To fill you up? Make you whole? To keep a promise? To respond to your requests? To be your Savior? As gentle as I can be, here is the truth.

They can't.

They were not created for any of those purposes.

God gives you the grace every day to be free of unrealistic expectations – theirs and yours. You can stop being hard on yourself for not being the "perfect wife" and stop being hard on your husband for not meeting your unrealistic expectations. Romans 12:2 here girls!

Do not conform any longer to the pattern of this world,
but be transformed by the renewing of your mind.
Then you will be able to test and approve what God's will is
his good, pleasing, and perfect will.

We are learning here I know. Transforming our minds and pushing out what the world tells us is okay, all so we can show the world what our great God can do in our marriage. Gentleness is a fruit of the Spirit and the He is ready to lay it on you. Ask for it. When I say "ask", I mean you should probably go begging for it and receive it with a spirit of expectation. Practice it. I promise, you will see your marriage begin to take deep root and flourish. Be gentle with it.

DAY 11: JUST A TOUCH

Ecclesiastes 9:10 says "*Whatever your hand finds to do, do it with all you might.*"

When I studied on this verse I began to feel as though it should have been written for Day 1 of this study. When you decided to do this study, you may have thought that it was a good "idea" to do a marriage study. I beg you to take this verse to heart and give your marriage your full attention. Decide now to get rid of all distractions that might make you lose focus on the "work" at hand. Today and every day for the rest of your life you will be glad you did.

What are your current distractions? Don't just think about them, write them down. Look them dead in the eye and tell them "no more!" Your marriage needs you to identify the things that are keeping your mind and thoughts busy but are also not necessary. Could it be social media? Maybe it is other relationships? How about trying to be super mom? Might it be your checking account? Whatever your distractions are, give them a name and a place to go. You truly need to spend some time studying on Biblical marriage and in prayer without distractions. If you're going to have a marriage that you can honestly say you've given "all your might" to, you need to address the things that are hindering you.

Whatever your hand finds to do... do it with all your might.

Philippians 4: 12 - 13 "I have learned the secret of being content in any and every situation, whether well fed or hungry, whether living in plenty or in want. I can do everything through him who gives me strength." NIV

No marriage is without sacrifice or compromise. No marriage is without hurt or pain. No marriage is without wounds and scars.

"If only I can reach him, if only I can touch the hem of his cloak..." there was so much focus and intention in what this woman was doing. With everything she had in her, she was reaching. No one could do it but her. No one could do it for her. She had to be the one who touched him. So much pain in her life was moving her closer to the One who could heal. Only she could do it, no one was willing to help get her there. The crowd was thick and heavy but with all her might she knew she needed just one touch. She knew no one could heal what she needed healing for and only the power of Jesus encountered personally would be her miracle. She had suffered for 12 years alone. No one knew just how deep her heartache was. No one understood her despair and she could depend on no one to bring her to this moment. She had to do it herself.

Oh ladies, how great was her faith that day. How great was her faith in what Jesus could do and she knew she only needed a touch to be changed? She believed. If this didn't work, she had no other options. She understood the source of the power. She had been to doctors, therapist, consulted friends and family, took advice from her priest, and all those efforts had let her down. However, when she laid her eyes on Jesus and witnessed His miracles firsthand, she knew He was the One. She was not afraid by those surrounding him. She could care less what the crowds would say, she needed Jesus. She just needed to touch his hem, she did, she was healed.

Could this be your story? Could this be you? Your marriage has suffered, you have done all you know to do. You've taken the advice of others, you've consulted so many people but in the end the healing has not happened where it was supposed to happen. It's time to step out in faith, reach for Jesus and believe that a touch of the One whose power breathes life into the stars will heal your marriage.

Experience Him.

Matthew 9:20-22, Mark 5:25-34, Luke 8:43-48

Ephesians 1:11-12 says "*In him we were also chosen (or made heirs, adopted), having been predestined according to the plan of him who works out everything in conformity with the purpose of his will in order that we, who were the first to hope in Christ, may be for the praise of his glory.*"

You cannot read those verses and not believe that God wants your marriage to be for His glory. He wants to heal. You are His and belong to Him, made an heir, adopted, chosen. He wants the very best for you. What He desires more than anything is for you to seek His face. To love Him first. To believe that He has the power to heal your marriage with just one touch and so, if you have never before sought Jesus with all your might, seek Him now. It's perfectly okay to seek Him solely for the belief of what His power can do with one touch. Jesus felt the power leave himself the day that suffering woman touched Him. She was healed by her belief. Your marriage can be totally and completely healed, restored, and redeemed by your belief.

And in him you too are being built together to become a dwelling in which God lives by his Spirit. -Ephesians 2:22

DAY 12: YOU ARE NOT ALONE

For this reason, and because of angels, the woman ought to have a sign of authority on her head. -1 Corinthians 11:10

I was reminded while praying over this study that I am not alone. The thing is, when you pray and then seek God in His Word, he reveals himself. The words come alive and it's as if He is truly speaking to you.

After the babies all went to bed, after my husband was asleep, I found myself in my prayer closet/laundry room. Nothing but a candle was lighting the room. I pray for so much wisdom. I pray for your marriage. I pray for your wisdom. I thank God for this opportunity and all His gifts. During this particular prayer I was thanking Him for giving me my husband. Something I encourage you to do is write out attitudes of your husband that you find godly. I pray over my husband's. When we met 27 years ago he was not a believer. He had lost his daddy at a young age and never quite resolved his grief. Now, as a man of faith, his faith is unwavering. He is steady and consistent in everything he does. His faith doesn't change or waiver. He believes every single thing happens for a reason. He is unchanging in how he loves his family. These are what make him a great man of God. All the other things that he is not, are of little importance with this type of perspective. This is why I encourage you to write down your husband's godly attributes. Begin to see your husband the way God intended him to be seen. See further, see where God wants to take him. I thanked God for being an unchanging God. This is a characteristic that I can depend on. After Amen, I sat down, opened my Bible. It opened straight to Malachi.

I the Lord do not change. Malachi 3:6

I could not have found that verse if I tried, not in a million tries of just opening my Bible would I have landed on that verse. The only one highlighted on that page. This is how the Holy Spirit lets you know He is helping you. This is how you know your Father is near. He speaks so blatantly through His Word when you seek Him. You are not alone, and He wants you to know.

Our days are filled with so much. We are juggling many balls and wearing many hats. It's a struggle. We struggle to get the kids to school on time, to work on time and to get home on time. If you're at all like me, a schedule helps you feel in control. Our schedules fill up with projects, chores, meals, and bills to be paid. We struggle with returning emails, phone calls, texts; we may, just maybe, have that same approach with our prayer time, our time with God. In the middle of our mess, it's difficult to make it all fit.

God wants to be near us. We don't always want God to fit in our schedule. The truth is, He doesn't expect us to do it alone and He certainly doesn't expect your willpower to be of any use in the matter. The truth is, His desire to be near us will override our desire to fit Him in. In all honesty, at the end of the day, with all the things that have gone wrong, all the things you did wrong, do you feel like He wants to spend time with you? In the middle of my mess, I don't feel worthy. Sometimes it's hard to open our lips and start speaking to Him. He's heard it all before, we mumble, and ramble and we just figure He is tired of hearing it all. The truth is, He wants it all.

God wants to be with you. Jeremiah 31:33-34 declares that the Lord will "put my law in their minds and write it on their hearts. I will be their God, and they will be my people. No longer will a man teach his neighbor or a man his brother, saying, 'Know the Lord,' because they will all know me, from the least to the greatest...For I will forgive their wickedness and will remember their sins no more." Praise Jesus, Amen.

He's taking the initiative. Our God, is just taking the wheel on our relationship with Him. One way or another, we are going to know He is God. He wants you to have a life that is abundant and free in Him. He has good things waiting for you and your husband. He wants you to have them so badly that He is going to write it on your hearts, so you'll never be without Him. The pace of your day affects your relationship with God. How? What are you doing or not doing to seek a relationship with Him? He is with you otherwise and in spite of. Isn't it a beautiful thing that our Father wants to be with you. He is patiently waiting right with you. He seeks you out.

In the middle of your hurry. In the middle of your pushing. In the middle of your work. He isn't waiting on your schedule to open up for Him. He has already come to you. Will your respond to His desire for you? Acknowledge His presence. Recognize the truth already written by Him on your heart. Rest in His presence, experience His power, feel His great love, and forgiveness.

In order to get our marriage right, to get it on back on track, to keep it moving forward, we must work on our relationship with the Father. We are of no use to our husbands if we keep relying on our own abilities and strengths. We tire out and become discouraged by the weight of the world and the swirling of our mess. Only He can make it all beautiful.

Remember, He is unchanged,

DAY 13: THE HELPER

As I was preparing for this day's study I back tracked all the way to the beginning. Something inside me just wanted to know more about the first lady, the very first wife according to God's Word.

Genesis 2:18 says "I will make him a comparable helper."

When I read the verse my immediate thought went straight to Jesus. He told all of us he would send another helper. (see John 14:16) God Himself would send His Spirit to help us. When we see the word "helper" here it is describing function rather than worth. I also looked up the scripture in various text and found that the word comparable was substituted for the words below...

- suitable
- just right
- fit for him
- help meet
- complement
- authority that is corresponding
- corresponds.

According to the scriptures, as wives, we are a comparable partner in assuming responsibilities during our life journey with our husbands. Notice the word equal was not used.

The reality is, the world has worked mightily to change the truth of our power as wives to our husbands. There is great power in knowing the truth of our roles as wives. Saying "yes" in a marriage ceremony isn't just saying so to get married and call him your husband, it's saying "yes' to God's divine plan as a helper, a wife.

In the same way, the Spirit helps us in our weakness. We do not know what we ought to pray for, but the Spirit himself intercedes for us with groans that words cannot express. Romans 8:26-27

Imagine how much we rely on the Spirit himself. We need Him. It is essential that we have the Spirit to intercede on our behalf. The Spirit always knows what is just right for us and knows when He is needed. The same goes for us as wives, as helpers. We can intercede in prayer for our husbands and our marriage. We can ask God to help us to know when we are most needed and to know how to handle situations in our marriage. Being a helper to us does not make the Spirit less important. Being our Helper is the most important gift from Christ that we have as Believers. Remember, you are a good thing for your husband and give him favor with the Lord.

Let's get to the heart of the conversation and strip away the idea or feeling that a helper is somehow less. Let's use the example of a physical task of lifting a log. On one end of a log is a man who is lifting, dragging, pulling, fighting, and struggling with the log. He begins to tire and feel the task is just too much. Then, along comes a helper who lifts the other end. The helper helps him carry, maneuver, place, and set the log until the task is complete. The helper made the job easier, right? It was less stressful and perhaps even enjoyable if the helper was good company to be around. They can celebrate the triumph over a heavy obstacle or even move to the next, accomplishing much more work at a comfortable pace that is probably just more enjoyable because of the companionship.

Did you imagine the helper as another man or as his wife? Either way, the same exact logic applies to your role as helper to your husband. You do make life better, easier for him. In turn, your reward comes with respect, love, appreciation, etc. Even if you don't always feel it or even if it's not recognized for what it is. God sees and knows your heart and will honor the help you offer.

As Christian wives, when we are troubled and find it difficult to pray, the Holy Spirit will intercede for us with a divine intensity (groans) that will express our needs perfectly to God. Believe that when you enter the throne room of your Father in prayer that your prayer is heard either from your heart or from your lips. He will honor your prayers for your marriage and your husband. He will give you direction on how to better help him and will encourage you. He will minister to your heart when your heart is in His

Will, with the desire to have Him more involved in your marriage. Invite Him in to lead and direct your heart on the matter of your love for your husband and your marriage.

As our husband's helper we are to be just that, a helper and not to be a hindrance. Becoming a hindrance to our husbands by not helping, putting them down, by nagging, or picking fights also hinders the blessings. The reality is, our husbands are not perfect, they can't do all that they are created to do without us. We aren't servants, we are helpers; we should be equally yoked. Your husband isn't meant to walk this journey of life alone. He is meant to walk it with you. I encourage you to reflect on your role and take notice of all the little things YOU do that are a blessing. Those little blessings you bring are magnified when we praise our Lord Father for allowing us to be a blessing.

But if we hope for what we do not yet have, we wait for it patiently. - Romans 8: 25

Do you hope for a better marriage? Do you hope for a marriage that is strong and lasting? Do you hope for a marriage that is full of love and desire? Do you hope...? Wait patiently. Ask the Spirit to pour His character of patience and long suffering out on you when needed. Hope in the promise that you and your husband will have the marriage your God dreams for you.

DAY 14: CREATED

Out of the ground God created every beast & bird; even Adam... Genesis 2:19

Woman was different. She was created from LIFE. The first mother, who would create and carry life was herself from life. One man, also became one woman. I am focusing all my attention on the significance of Genesis 2:19-23 today.

I wanted to focus here on the significance of woman not being created like all the others. She was created from man, for him. A perfect partner.

Adam said, "bone of my bone, flesh of my flesh" (v 23) He stood astonished and amazed. Go back to the list of words God used to describe his comparable helper.

- suitable
- just right
- comparable
- fit for him
- help meet
- compliment
- corresponding

"Equal" was not one of those words. They weren't the same, they were different, but they fit together, they complimented each other. God made each animal unique and he made them with mates. He knew Adam would need a helper, but He also knew she would be the most unique creature of all His creation. She was going to be the first created from life.

It is believed in some doctrines that Adam himself possessed characteristics of both man and woman. When God took from Adam, he took the feminine part. We aren't talking physical parts necessarily, we are talking about emotions and our nature as women. It's believed that the naming of all the animals had a feminine influence. Consider this, the influence was done so without inhibiting Adam from his task of naming. It was simply an influence, one that was so great it is demonstrated even today in the language of other cultures.

He took away from Adam to give him Eve, creating his feminine counterpart as a walking, breathing, loving woman and leaving him with the masculine.

All that to say...you my friend, were never an afterthought.

There are many analogies for the significance of taking from Adam and creating a woman. Let's focus on what this means for you, as a wife. It is simple. God dreamed you up. He knitted you together with each fiber of your being. He created you for a purpose. Being a wife to your husband is part of His plan. He created you! He created you for a purpose and part of your purpose as a wife, is to be a wife.

If you believed God would create the perfect wife for your husband, do you believe you are his perfect, comparable companion? If God had laid your husband down in a deep sleep, would He have pulled a rib from him and created you? Your answer is "Yes!" Even if you feel differently, the truth is "Yes".

...he who created the heavens and stretched them out, who spread out the earth and all that comes from it, who gives breath to its people, and life to those who walk on it; I the Lord have called you to righteousness. I will take hold of your hand. I will keep you and will make you to be a covenant and a light. -Isaiah 42: 5 & 6

Oh sister, isn't that just beautiful. He created all of the things we need to survive and flourish. He breathed life into us and gave our eyes a vision of beauty in the heavens to awe us. He puts the ground beneath our feet so that we will know He is who He is. All of this and more just to call you to righteousness. He will hold your hand and make you to be a promise and a light. You are this to the world when you draw yourself close to Him and you are these things to your husband. He put within you the power to "*open the eyes of the blind, to free captives from prison and to release those that sit in darkness.*" -Isaiah 45:7

Because of Jesus, we have this power. We can, with the power of the Holy Spirit given to us by our Jesus, we can open our husband's eyes when he is blind to truth, when he is captive and held prisoner to sin, and when he sits in darkness we can be his light.

You, sister, were created to be the perfect compatible, comparable counterpart to your husband. Do you ever feel that is not true? Do you believe the devil is always out to discredit God's Truth? Don't you for a second believe Satan's lies! As hard as it is to perfectly love, you were still created to be everything your imperfect husband needs. With marriage you have to put feelings aside sometimes, put circumstances aside, and look truth right in the eye.

O people in Zion, inhabitants in Jerusalem, you shall weep no more. He will be very generous to you at the sound of your cry. When He hears it. He will answer you. - Isaiah 30:9

Your Creator hears you.

If He can take dust and water and create life, if He can create something out of nothing, imaging what He can do with your marriage just as it is right now.

He hears you.

DAY 15: FULLNESS

"...He brought her to the man." -Genesis 2:22

Can you even imagine what it must have been like for Eve? Her very first experience was in the presence of God. She saw Him first. God, in all His Glory, was all she needed and known, nothing less. He created her, understood her, cherished her, loved her every fiber and yet, He walked her right up to Adam and gave her away. Everything she had ever known about love and life was perfect and full. Now this glorious woman was standing face to face with man, her man, her counterpart. I'm sure she didn't also know he would behave like a man, treat her differently than God, she had no idea the difference. Man's love would be different than God's. She doesn't know yet that his love will be less than and flawed from what she had already experienced.

From the fullness of his grace we have all received one blessing after another. -John 1:16

Grace is "the kindness and the love of God our Savior" ...not because of righteous things we have done. God hears our righteous prayers and answers them. This is why it is important to lift your husband and marriage up in prayer with your voice. With fervent, audacious, and bold prayers you are being called to speak over your marriage. Your prayers are empowered, and it is your responsibility to speak them to the Father, the possibilities that are set into motion with prayer will cause your marriage to receive one blessing after another. By His grace! By the fullness of His grace you will receive based on His love for you and your husband.

God's love for us is perfect and we cannot compare it to anything here on earth. Christ's love for his church, his people, is one we strive for. At this moment in time, Eve and Adam are untarnished and probably are in awe of one another. Eve will step away from her Father's arms into the loving arms of man. I can't even fathom that. Can you? I know when my Daddy gave me away at our wedding I was going to miss him so much but had to trust my new husband could be the man I needed him to be, as best as he could. Do husbands disappoint? Do they come into marriage knowing exactly what to do? They fall short. Just like we do as wives. It's a lifetime of learning how to live together. Does our marriage sometimes leave us feeling hopeless? Sure, it does. Can our husbands be better men? Can they be more? Can they be that comparable companion that meets at least some of our needs. Yes! We aren't studying on them ladies. We are studying on our role as wives and how to improve our marriage and what we have to work with can seem like the pits or we can learn and nurture it and make it beautiful. We have that power.

So why not ask? Our God is limitless and so are the possibilities. Our intercession for our marriage in prayer allows God to give us a vision from a heavenly perspective. What is your marriage saying to the world? The world begins to see that it is not one that fulfills the other but that God, in His perfect fullness, completes us as individuals where our flesh fails. We are to pray for change in every aspect of our marriage, and our lives, so that we are seeking to be complete in Christ and not each other.

Where we tend to fall short is that we are guilty of seeking our own fullness in our husbands. We need them to love us a certain way. We may crave more kindness, more touch, more sweet words, more gifts, and I could go on and on. The reality is, our fullness is found in Christ Jesus alone. We can't be their everything and they can't be ours. Only the God that created us out of complete love can fill us and satisfy. Our husbands cannot be given that great responsibility of pleasing and satisfying our every need. They cannot possibly meet our expectations on their own. They need Christ and so do you.

Our frustrations with our husbands will always come from their inability to fulfill our expectations.

What do you do about this? You pray, and you seek your fullness from God. The Father made you to seek Him, Christ will lay down everything to win you, and the Spirit is calling out to help you. He will put your expectations in perspective.

DAY 16: UNITY

"This is now bone of my bones
And flesh of my flesh...
Genesis 2:23

Amazed? Relieved. Excited! Adored.

What must have Adam thought of this beautiful creature standing before him on the Father's arm? One thing is certain, he recognized immediately that she was from him. His thoughts could have possibly gone something like this....

"She is of me. She gets me. She understands me. She will know my strengths and weaknesses. She feels my pain and my hurt. She will help me seek relief and rest when I need it. She'll be fun to be around. We can explore the garden together."

I was sitting in church listening to a sermon from a guest preacher, but my mind was going back towards this study I wanted to work on. So, I opened up my journal and started scribbling thoughts and verse and just trying to open up to the lesson God wanted me to learn that day. My husband was sitting next to me watching. He's always gets to witness the Spirit move after I do a Bible study, read, or discuss a new revelation, or sometimes even when I write something down and it later is more significant than we realized at the time. That's the Spirit and today was no exception. I had just written the sentences below when something happened that made us both take a breath and smile.

She is tuned to her husband. That isn't as easy for us these days as wives but it's important to be aware of it. We were created to be in tune with our husband, whom we love.

Not 5 minutes after I wrote this thought down did our preacher say the words below.

Just like when tuning pianos, the tuner uses 1 fork. Thousands of pianos will be tuned to just 1 fork. So, they are tuned to each other.

He went on about how beautiful the sound is when many piano's play together that have been tuned by the same fork. Just like we are to be tuned to our husbands, we are also to be tuned to the Holy Spirit to be unified.

These word choices that God had given me and our guest preacher that day were not by chance. We were tuned to the Spirit. The Spirit will always show up and show unity in your life when you turn your heart to God. Unity is what we seek. Understanding of each other's needs that runs so deep we meet them before we realize we have.

We all seek to be understood. We all want nothing more than for our husbands to understand us. But first, we must learn to understand them (and maybe even ourselves). Just as Adam knew that they were tuned to each other, your goal in your marriage is to be tuned as well. Unity in your marriage, that is tuned to the Holy Spirit, allows for your marriage to reflect God's beautiful plan for families. Pray and prepare for unity because God is about to do something great.

Ephesians 4:2-5 says *with all lowliness and gentleness, love, endeavoring to keep the unity of the Spirit in the bond of peace. There is one body and one Spirit, just as you were called in one hope of your calling; one Lord, one faith, one baptism, one God and Father of all, who is above all and through all, and in you all.*

You don't have to worry about how the unity will happen. You simply need to pray for it.

Speaking of prayer, this is the part that matters most. This is the part that God really wants you to focus. There will come a time in your marriage when it is critical that you pray. Many lose hope and believe that failures are irreversible. They are not. Write down all the things you are praying for and "nail" them to your wall. Put them in a place where you can pray and spend time with Him and pray over them. Sometimes answered prayers don't always look like answered prayers at first so keep trusting. Sometimes in the hidden places we cannot see is were God is working His biggest miracles. Psalm 2:8 tells us that if we ask Him, He will give us the nations of our inheritance and the ends of the earth for our possessions. Will He not give you the thing you are praying for most in your marriage? Pray for the unity that you seek in your marriage. Unity is what marriage was designed to be unified. Look for aspects in your relationship, life, work, time, etc. that need more unity. We all seek to be understood and our husbands are no different. We are no different.

And over all these virtues put on love, which binds them all together in perfect unity. - Colossians 3:14

DAY 17: HE HAS A PLAN

God's plan for marriage is given and repeated in the Gospels and in the Epistles. (Gen 2:24, Matt 19:5, Eph. 5:31.) As we all know, God's plan is not always our plan. Marriage, as God's plan, is perfect in its organization; one man and one woman in a lifetime commitment. Frankly, that's asking a lot. That's a big commitment for life, to spend life with just one husband in all our flaws and flesh.

The marriage covenant has 3 parts according to Gen 2:24.

1. The husband to leave his father and mother.
2. To be united (holding fast or clinging).
3. To become one flesh

Adam and Eve...God introduced them himself and then established a bond. He wanted to ensure they stayed together, forever and always. A tight bond that would hold them together through good times and bad. He established this for your marriage as well. Although in many marriages this 3-prong approach is not 3 pongs. Some are just 2 or maybe even 1 and a collapse is waiting to happen. Knowing these things to be true, as scripture is true, it gives us something specific to work on and pray for.

As a mother of boys, it breaks my heart to say, but one day each of my sons, as they marry, will leave our care and join their wives. We will always and forever, God willing, be here for them but we're are not called to provide or make decisions concerning their new life together. We are to simply to equip, set an example, and pray. We are to be here for them if needed but expect them to consult their wives and not us with matters concerning their marriage. Our sons will leave, and they will honor us to do so. They will always know where to find us.

We are to be united as I talked about in yesterday's devotion and become one flesh. We will discuss this soon. If any of these three truths are out of place in your marriage, it is time to pray for rectification. John 14:13-14 says that "I will do whatever you ask in My name that the Father may be glorified in the Son. If you ask anything in My name, I will do it." That is a powerful promise.

I remember when my husband and I were first engaged, that my future mother-in-law told me that she was sad, she'd be losing her son. Of course, I said "don't be ridiculous" but she said, the son is supposed to leave his mother and cleave to his wife. Now, after 17 years I understand what she meant. It wasn't that he was "leaving" her for good but that he would come to need and respect what I could provide as his wife. I might not make my carrot cake like his Momma did, but he still loves my carrot cake. He wouldn't dare compare. He doesn't call his Mom if we have a fight or a difference of opinion, he calls me. We work it out with each other or we work it out in our prayer closets. When we first got married we built a house not far from my parents. My Mom told me that when they built their house, not far from my grandparents (Dad's parents) that my Granny and Papaw never bothered them and stayed out of their business. They were there if they were needed. It was out of respect that they did and out of love that they let them be, but they were there for them if needed. So, after seeing this passed down through the generations, I have to say, I see why it is important for husband and wife to cleave to each other. It builds a stronger relationship when you work on your own marriage. It allows you to fully cling to one another.

To be joined and become one flesh seem like the same statement. Joining however involves the joining of life, responsibilities, finances, etc. One flesh involves intimacy not related to the other. Different couples have different opinions on what should be shared and what should be kept separate. They may share bills but not bank accounts or bank accounts and bills. The point is, that there is a joining of life and responsibilities. My husband and I believe in the what's his is mine and what's mine is his. That's what works for us. We share everything. We don't have the "it's my car, house, money, etc." outlook. Everything is "it's ours", no matter whose name is signed on the dotted line. It works for us and what works for us may look different for your marriage.

Intimacy generally isn't as hard for most. It's usually the one thing we get right in the beginning but sometimes, not. Some couples struggle with this. Some struggle with the commitment of monogamy and staying faithful. However, it is usually the prong that makes or breaks the marriage. Remaining intimate and loving towards each other can become hard. We all go through times when we don't feel like we did towards each other in the beginning. These times just need a reset button. You go back to focusing on why you loved a person to begin with, what changed, why it's different, and what can you do now to light a new spark in your marriage.

One unit, working together. This is the unit that Satan works the hardest at tearing apart. The bonds should seem impossible for him to break but he uses a carefully planned strategy to break the unit. God never intended for man to be alone. The very bone which He made woman came from man himself. There were no parents in Eden, but God was not speaking to the present, He was speaking to the future. We are to lay aside our old loyalties and lifestyles for a new plan. One that goes from separate dreams and goals to joined dreams and goals with unconditional commitment and love. This combined unit will be strong and lasting. No other relationship, even that of mother and child, is to surpass that of a husband and wife. Marriage is a threefold miracle.

I remember a time when my husband and I struggled with a prong or two. However, through prayer and open hearts we persevered and on the other side, when we looked up, we saw we really do have the marriage we dreamed of. Pray and pray for open hearts. Pray for healing and give God praise for what He is about to do. Praise Him.

DAY 18: HAPPINESS GAP

In 2009, when I first wrote this devotion there was a new study out called <u>You Can't Be Happier than Your Wife: Happiness Gaps and Divorce.</u> All these years later and these findings are still true. When I read this article, I was surprised at many details I would have never considered. Did you know that 2/3's of all divorces filed, are filed by the wife? Did you know that when the wife did most of the housework, if her income was higher than her husbands or if they were from different social backgrounds, then the divorce rate was higher? Fear not, desperate housewives your marriage isn't doomed, neither is the successful business woman's or those of different backgrounds. As a matter of fact, in the marriages where the woman was a housewife or student, chores where shared, and/or backgrounds where similar, things were looking pretty sunny not a cloud in the sky.

What the study suggests is that too large of a "happiness gap" is what spurs on a divorce. Now, that I get. It's not about the housework, the money or social background differences, it's simply about happiness. It seems to me that because it is women that are filing for divorce at a much higher rate than men, means only one thing...the men are happy, and they didn't think divorce was necessary. They still think they can fix all things.

What about us women? When that happiness gap gets bigger and bigger we don't know how to close it. We throw our hands up and say, "I'm over it!" Right? Well, the way I see it, if you are still hanging in here with me, you haven't thrown your hands up, you aren't "over it" and you are willing to close the gap so that you and your husband are both equally happy.

Now, this study only gives worldly suggestions to how to solve the problem, like sharing responsibilities, giving equal time to responsibilities, etc. It also tells us that we should be careful about "keeping score". We should be careful when thinking that responsibilities should be shared equally. Keeping score can lead to resentment. What it suggests to me is that communication is critical because expectations can simply go unnoticed. Asking for help in a nice way is going to always be much better than complaining that your husband "never helps out."

What the study doesn't tell us is that we have a manual that is written to perfection as a guide to our happiness. You guessed it, God's Holy Word, our divine Bibles have the answer.

Give me your heart...and let your eyes delight in my ways. -Proverbs 23:26

"Delight", I love that word. It makes my whole outlook seem brighter. In order to be happy, we need to find delight in one another and the things we do for each other. To find happiness in my marriage is what is at the top of my list. I want to be happy when I am a friend to my husband, I want to be happy when I fold his clothes, I want to be happy when we have time to spend with our children, I want to be happy!!!

My husband is the first to say, "our marriage isn't broken, what's to fix". He's happy! However, I'm the one that finds myself crying sometimes because he doesn't have time to talk to me during the work day or goes to sleep as soon as he hits the pillow, instead I should be happy he is willing to work so hard. I could rattle down a whole list of reasons why I need to be happy but instead, I need to apply what I already know and start being happy with where my marriage is headed. I am delighted that God has a plan for us!

The good news is, that if you have a happiness gap, God has what you need to close it. It may take a bit of shameless persistence to close that gap, but it will be worth it. Luke 11:5-10 is the parable of a persistent friend. Matt 7:7 has the same message. Ask. Seek. Knock.

For everyone who asked receives; he who seeks finds; and to him who knocks, the door will be opened. -Luke 11:10

If you want to know the first step and most important secret to closing your happiness gap, the above scripture is it.

Drop something you normally feel you need to do and spend time in prayer for your marriage. Ask for happiness. Seek happiness. Bang on Heavens gates for happiness. God will give, show you, and open up the possibilities. Also, take a moment to find delight in your husband for the sake of your happiness.

The Lord will continually guide you and satisfy your desire. – Isaiah 58:11

DAY 19: TIME STARVED

If two lie down **together** *they keep warm, but how can one be warm alone?* -Ecclesiastes 4:11

Time spent together is vital to the health of a marriage. Without spending time together, we can't share, laugh, cry or enjoy each other's company. When the opportunity arises for us to spend time with our spouse and we don't, our marriages become resentful, stagnate and sometimes even die. As obvious as this fact seems, many marriages today are time starved. They are time starved, touch starved, and dream starved. When we don't take time for one another we begin missing out on the elements of life that connect us. Human touch is vital to our wellbeing. Communicating our hopes and dreams is vital to prosper. If we were to put dots on our marriage time line of all the moments we spent time with our husbands, would our time line become like a beautiful string of pearls or would it be full of gaps and piecing pieces?

God's Holy Word, that is alive, is calling us to spend time with Him. In doing so, we then spend time in prayer. It's essential, we speak to our Father and He speaks to us through His Word. His Spirit moves, and the communication is made complete. This is an example of our marriage should be. It is a structure that is in place for perfect communion with the Lord. Jesus Christ made the way for this to be possible. He wants no less for your marriage.

And over all these virtues put on **love**, *which binds them all* **together** *in perfect unity.* *Colossians 3:13-15*

Usually a lack of time spent together is simply a matter of poor planning or we just aren't really good at saying "no" to those that want commitments from us. When our commitments start to outweigh our available time, aspects of our marriage start to suffer. We are all surrounded by people that demand our time; employers, kids, church, school, etc. If you happen to have a husband that doesn't speak up, he's liable to end up at the bottom of the list. The flip side is if a spouse is too vocal, they are often accused of being selfish, manipulative, controlling, etc. We simply cannot let aspirations for our life negatively affect our relationship with our loved ones. Just as they should not negatively affect our relationship with Christ.

Love *and faithfulness meet* ***together****; righteousness and peace kiss each other.* -Psalm 85:9-11

It really doesn't matter why couples find themselves not spending enough time together; what does matter, is that it is a problem that is recognized and remedied. Spending time together should be high on the priority list and it should stay there. Your marriage could depend on it. In order to gain more time with your husband, start by devoting more time to prayer. Ask God to show you what our time means to Him. Ask God reveal to you what is missing from your marriage that time spent together can remedy. It may just be that it is time for you both to dream again, to learn to love again, or simply to adore the presence of one another.

Plan a date night, lunch or romantic evening, just the two of you. Leave all distractions behind and dedicate time together. It's important to stick to it. Make time spent together a priority.

DAY 20: REACH THE HEART

Well friends, we are half way through this study. If you've made it this far I am giving you a heads up, the next 10 days will be the most challenging. After day 30 you will be able to look up and see the difference these many days of prayer and studying God's Word has made on your marriage. You may even already see a difference. I encourage you to keep running this race until you reach the flourishing end. Today we are going to start in Colossians.

Let the peace of Christ rule in your hearts, since as members of one body you are called to walk in peace. -Colossians 3:15

Does peace rule in your marriage? It's a simple question but I want you to be honest. Do you feel as though you are always in the middle of a mess? Does chaos seem like part of your everyday? I am here to tell you that our Father has something much better. Jesus came to us to bring us something special.

A friend of mine pulled me aside one day after a good cry I was having and told me a story. I had heard the story before but let me share it with you too. She said, "remember the Bible story about Jesus and his disciples in the boat during the storm. The waves were crashing, and the disciples were afraid. They went to Jesus in a panic, not believing he could calm the storm, and woke him from his peaceful nights rest for fear they were about to drown. When they did, Jesus got up, calmed the storm and when all was calm he turned and said, 'Where is your faith?' They were shocked. The could not believe that even the wind and rain obeyed Him." (Luke 8:22-25) My friend said, "just get in the bottom of the boat with Jesus and lay next time him in peace". Whoa! Point taken.

Jesus was ruled by peace. His heart was never in fear of the storm. He could sleep straight through it with no fear of drowning. He paid it no mind. Jesus said...

Peace I leave with you; my peace I give you. I do not give to you as the world gives. Do not let your hearts be troubled, do not be afraid. -John 14:27

I have told you these things, so that in Me you may have peace. In this world you will have trouble. BUT take heart, I have overcome the world. -John 16:3

Jesus says all this. We get the impression that He came to this world to hand out peace freely like tossing gold coins in the air, we would collect it like the treasure it is. However, Jesus wants you to know that the peace He gives is actually a Sword. He wasn't bringing you peace, He was bringing you the power to receive your peace in such a way that it was a weapon for the enemy.

What started this whole search for answers on peace and the sword? During my study time I followed a few side notes around in my Bible before landing on ...

Do not suppose that I have come to bring you peace to the earth, I did not come to bring peace, but a sword. -Matt 10:24

What? Wait a minute. I thought all that talk about having peace for myself was just a given. It was just handed over to me. Boy, was I wrong. Jesus said some things too that made me keep digging...

For all who draw the sword will die by the sword. -Matt 26:25

What is your weapon? When there is a struggle in your marriage, when you are fighting, when you're not speaking, when you are pushing buttons...what is your weapon? Ephesians 6:17 instructs us to use one weapon and one only. The Sword of the Spirit.

The Sword of the Spirit cuts through the mess and the chaos. It is sharper than a double edge sword. The sword is both offensive and defensive. It is a weapon belonging to the Holy Spirit. It is used to protect and defend. I don't know about you but if I am trying to rescue my marriage or learn to be a more prayerful wife I want something at my disposal that I can use to defend and protect. However, with such a weapon comes a great amount of training. You have to know how to handle your Sword (Word of God, the Holy Scriptures) 2

Timothy 3:16-17

The Sword is used offensively to demolish evil strongholds in our marriage. It is used offensively to correct errors and falsehoods that have been spoken over our marriage. 2 Corinthians 10:4 & 5 tells us that the Word is living and active. The Sword is double edged. When a sword is double edged it has the ability to cut in every way, to easily penetrate. It reaches straight to the heart. Knowing this, I go all the way back to Matt 26:25. For all who draw the Sword (or live by the Sword), die by the Sword. What that means is...

We will open God's Word daily and die to our self.

Dying to oneself is a concept that can be hard to understand. If you are struggling with this, maybe I can help. To die to self is simply the act of setting aside what we desire in that moment and focus instead on loving God with our whole hearts. We value others as much as we value ourselves. (Matt 22: 37-39) We are no longer focused on our self and self-centeredness but are open hearted, ready to follow Christ who cares more deeply for others. Matt 16:24 is where Jesus explains that we must deny ourselves (die to self) and take up our cross and follow Him.

The Sword of the Spirt, God's Holy Word will penetrate your heart, it will reach it and when it does, by simply opening His Word. You will die to self. In order to have the peace Jesus left for us, you must take up the Sword he brought to us.

To truly want what is best for your marriage you have to train yourself on how to handle such a powerful weapon. You will die to self-daily so that you can have the view Christ has for your marriage, for your husband.

You're in the army now ladies. The next 20 days will be full of God's Word and prayer to protect your marriage. You will be equipped, and your eyes opened. You will gain strength in Christ Jesus and become an influencer in your marriage through prayer.

Father, I cry out to You that you will make me a house of prayer for my marriage. I believe that within my identity of Christ I am to also be a peacemaker. Holy Spirit, fill me with Your knowledge and guide me through the Holy Word. Give me all that I need in wisdom and spiritual understanding. Lord, let me be a vessel that You can use for Your glory. Fill me up with all of You so that I will overflow with your glory onto my husband. Give me grace to become a laborer of prayer, believing in the release of Your power over our marriage, to win my husband to You, to give our marriage to You. All that is on earth belongs to You; revive my marriage and impact it with your gospel daily. As I yield to the Holy Spirit daily, teach me to pray. Give me an unbroken, focused spirit to intercede for my marriage. I offer my life to You. Let the days of my life and the days of my marriage serve Your will and purpose. In Jesus name, Amen

.

DAY 21: YOUR HELMET

Satan wants to attack the mind, the way he defeated Eve. (Genesis 3; 2 Corinthians 11:1-3) It's referred to as "the fall". It changes history. It takes place in the midst of a perfect paradise among sinless people. It all begins with Satan and his disguise. He was clever, shrewd, and cunning. The Bible never tells us why he approached Eve and not Adam, but we can all agree it is probably because God never told her of the prohibition directly, do not eat the fruit of the Tree of Knowledge. She had taken it at Adam's word and not God's direct word. The Devil began the entire conversation by questioning God in Genesis 3:3..."**but God did say, 'You must not eat fruit from the tree that is in the middle of the garden, and you must not touch it, or you will die.'" Here we can see that** Eve exaggerated God's command. Funny how those last two sentences are something we tend to do from time to time. We question God. We exaggerate His commands or just the opposite and ignore them completely. Usually exaggeration is used to make our God Father seem so unjust that we just can't possibly live out what He expects of us. Or the exaggeration is simply because it was not conveyed correctly to us by another. Either way, that is why it's important to read His Word for ourselves, He will speak directly to us.

Read Genesis 3:5

These words spoken by the serpent are just a straight up lies.. The entire temptation was tied up at the end with a perfect little lie. "...you will be like God, knowing good and evil." Being like God has nothing to do with knowing good and evil. God is good all the time because He *is* good. The temptation to be disobedient simply involved gaining knowledge without first being obedient. Proverbs 14:12 says that our ways may seem right, but our ways end in death. Every temptation is to go your own way and not God's way.

Genesis 3:6, the tree is attractive to the eye, appealing to the appetite, and enticing to ambition. Simply by listening to another creature rather than God means that they sinned. They believed his lie. In Genesis, it goes on that Adam denies responsibility (Gen 3:12), then Eve copied his response (v13) and God judges the serpent (v14). Later in Rev 12:9 the serpent is identified as having the intelligence of Satan. He is charming and deadly and represents opposition to God. Before passing judgement on Eve, we see the first prophesy of the Messiah (v15), notice God does not "curse" her like he does the serpent and Adam.

Satan does want to attack the mind. Christ defeated Evil. The Helmet of Salvation that we are about to discuss is a God given weapon. It refers to a mind controlled by God and His Truth.

The Helmet of Salvation (Is 59:17, Eph. 6:17, 1 Th 5:8) protects our minds from the world. As women and wives, it is important that we receive the responsibility of acquiring knowledge through His Word. Too many Christians have this idea that intellect is not important, when in reality it is a vital weapon against evil. It's essential to our Christian growth, service, and victory. When we dig into God's Truth and learn what God has to say in His Word, then He is able to control the mind, and if He controls our mind, Satan cannot lead His children astray. When Paul taught new Christians the truths of the Word of God, it was the helmet of their salvation that protected them from Satan's lies.

Take the helmet of salvation and the sword of the Spirit, which is the Word of God. - Ephesians 6:17

If we haven't been fitted with our helmet of salvation, then we are subject to be a casualty in battle.

For our struggle is not against flesh and blood (what you can see), but against the rulers, against the powers, against the world forces of the darkness, against the spiritual forces of wickedness in the heavenly places (what you can't see) -Ephesians 6:12 with additional comments)

Our salvation is our eternal security with Christ and the full inheritance promised to us that we have been given because of our relationship with

Him. It includes all our blessings, all of our status, and all of our identity. Everything from Him we have received enables us to live in victory for Him. When you choose to use this divine weapon of power you cut our enemy off before he has a chance to enter.

Put on your helmet of salvation.

Your salvation is a gift. There is no exact formula or fancy prayer that needs to be said in order to receive it. If you believe Christ, as the Son of God, died for you because of your sin, you only need ask Him for salvation. Ask Him for your helmet. He has it ready, it fits you perfectly and He's just waiting to place it on your head. You are always welcome to contact me, or you may be more comfortable seeking out a friend if you have questions, but the prayer is yours to say, the asking comes from your heart and your lips.

Ladies, your God given helmet is there. If you ever have questions about what thoughts might be going through your head, ask God to capture them and let no others enter. Your helmet might just need to be set back on straight. Remember always that you are an intelligent woman and your salvation is secure. No lies the Devil tries to tell you are to enter your thoughts.

While this devotional is about your personal armor, your armor is intended to be used in all areas of your life that need protecting. Our marriage is vital to the Kingdom of God. As we discussed previously, it was designed. It has a purpose in His Kingdom work and when you start putting on your armor, piece by God given piece, you will find that you are ready for when the enemy strikes at your marriage. All you need do is protect your husband and your marriage with the tools/armor God has provided. The Lord will guard you and fight for you. Remember the war has already been won, it's the battles that need conquering in our lives. It's the little battles the Devil wants to win. Don't let him. Don't let him have your marriage! Fight for it. Set your helmet on straight and lift your Sword!

The next few devotionals coming up will help you become fully equipped and ready for all battles if you don't already feel equipped. Know, that you have everything you need now.

Father, I come to you today and ask you to set my helmet of salvation on straight. Capture all thoughts that are not of You; lead me daily to Your truths and promises for me and for my marriage. Lord, protect my husband, help him to put on his armor every morning. Cover us in your grace and protection. Send out angel armies to stand guard against the evil one who seeks to destroy my marriage and relationship with my husband. Lord, reveal to me any aspect of my marriage that needs prayer and put a halt to all things within that are putting a block on our blessings. Holy Spirit, I ask that You intercede in my prayer and open my eyes. Unveil before me the things I cannot yet see so that I know where the attacks come from. Lord, expose the enemy and bring him into full view. Help me to see only what you need me to see. Keep my focus on Jesus. Blind me to the human drama, places, events, and people that can be seen because my battle is not with them. Lord, within my salvation is the power to defeat the evil. The won who is an imposter, whose wings you clipped on Calvary. The imposter does not stand a chance against me, my husband, or my marriage as I am clothing myself in Your armor. Amen

DAY 22: YOUR SHIELD

...take up the shield of faith, with which you can extinguish all the flaming arrows of the evil one. -Ephesians 6:16

You may already be familiar with the verse above, perhaps you even know how to take up your shield of faith. Can I take a you a bit further in scripture so your understanding of the shield has a fuller meaning.

...he is a shield to those who walk in blameless, for he guards the course of the just and protects the way of his faithful ones. -Proverbs 2:7-8

Every word of God is flawless; he is a shield to those who take refuge in him. - Proverbs 30:5

..."Do not be afraid, Abram. I am your shield, your very great reward." -Genesis 15:1

You are my refuge and my shield, I have put my hope in your word. - Psalm 119:114

Psalms is full of references of how our Father is our shield. So many of us refer to our shield of faith as something that involves our own strength, that it's power is dependent on our faith or lack thereof. What God's Word says over and over, is that He is our shield. He is where we draw our faith from. We have faith in Him and not of what we can do on our own. On our own a shield is heavy, on our own our shield is hard to carry, on our own our shield requires maintain and work to keep it sturdy and functional.

With God as our shield, our faith is unwavering. It may be heavy for us but for God we need only stand behind it.

With God as our shield, we have faith to move forward. With God as our shield, we have faith to get closer to the enemy with our Sword.

With God as our shield, we have faith that are protected. With God as our shield, we have faith that we are hidden from attacks.

With God as our shield, we have faith that He can give us rest during battle.

With God as our shield, we have faith that we are not alone.

With God as our shield, we have faith we are cared for and never forgotten.

With God as our shield, we have faith that the enemy will let down his own guard.

The shield was large, usually about 4 feet by 2 feet. It was made of wood and covered in tough leather. It as curved and polished so that it was slick. As the solider held it before him, it protected him from spears, arrows, and fiery darts. The edges were designed so that they could interlock with others and form a larger barrier against the enemy. This suggests that as Christians it is important to bring our Shield of Faith to battle when we meet together and that we do not battle alone. The faith mentioned here is not a "saving" faith, it is a living faith. It is trust in the promises and power of God.

Faith is a defensive weapon that protects us from Satan's fiery darts that are directed at our hearts and minds: lies, blasphemous thoughts, doubts, desire for sin, and hateful thoughts towards others. It is our faith that quenches these darts. We never know when the Devil will fire a dart but sure enough he is looking for an opportunity. He's look for you to let your guard down. This is why we must always walk by faith and use our God given shield

I can recall one particular time that my husband and I both let our guards down. We received such an attack that we didn't know if we could survive it. We were both so very wounded and hurt. Our brokenness was exposed and it all came at a time when we were walking the very path God had called us too. We are following direction from the Lord in our lives. One that changed the history and make up of our family simply because we stayed the course. We let God heal, we showed Him our wounds and battle scars. By His stripes, we were healed, our marriage was healed. We may have had our helmets on and our swords ready but without our shield the enemy gained entry into parts of us that hurt the deepest.

Our God is Mighty! He is loving and forgiving. Praise Jesus!

Our Heavenly Father would not tell us to not be afraid over and over if He didn't understand our nature of fear, worry, anxiety and how we get dry mouth, cold sweats, sweaty palms all wrapped up with a racing heartbeat whenever we are under attack. The Devil is fully aware of how we react in dire situations. This is why he is hiding and lurking, waiting for the perfect moment to attack. He's waiting for that moment when you say "I got this God. I'm good now."

God is always there. He is listening to your prayers for your marriage. He hears your cries for protection. He is ready to reaffirm to you His promises for your marriage and light the way in His direction. When you pray, it's your opportunity to lay wide open your fears so that He can cover them and protect you from them. His promises for your future are protected, He is your shield. Don't let your fears and mangled thoughts steer you off the path He has for you, call on Him to be your protector. Hit your knees and rest within Him when the battle is too much, when the arrows keep coming, hit your knees and let Him cover you with your shield of faith.

Father, I choose today to be a victor with Your as my protector. I refuse to be a victim of circumstances surrounding my marriage and in life. Lord, I lift my marriage and my husband up to you today so that you may cover them. Protect us from the fiery darts the Devil has seen fit to aim at us. Release your power and glory upon my husband and myself. I will raise my voice to You and enter Your Heavenly throne room until I see a revival in my marriage like no other. I will not be moved, afraid, or shaken. I will rest in You and beneath your protection. My shield of faith is You Father and all of your promises. Let the light of Your glory shine and flood our marriage so that others can see what is possible. Lord whatever adversity we face, help us face it together, help us to lock our shields and move forward during battle to slay the enemy and be overcome only by the power of Your love for us. Thank you, Jesus, Amen.

DAY 23: GOSPEL CENTERED

...and with your feet fitted with the readiness that comes with the gospel of peace. -Ephesians 6:15

I think this piece of armor may very well be my favorite to study. It's such a beautiful thing to read about. Often, when we talk about the feet being fitted we have the image of the sandals worn into battle, how they are sturdy leather with the spikes coming out of the bottom. They definitely aren't meant for style or comfort but are purely for function. However, when I read deeper into God's Word on the subject these are the words I love most.

...How beautiful are the feet of those who bring good news. -Romans 10:15

This verse is in reference to a scripture in Nahum.

Look, there on the mountains the feet of one who brings good news, who proclaims peace! - Nahum 1:15 and then they celebrated because those feet of peace mean that no more will they be invaded; the enemy has been destroyed completely.

Isaiah goes on to share...

How beautiful on the mountains are the feet of those who bring good news, who proclaim peace, who bring good tidings, who proclaim salvation, who say to Zion, "Your God reigns!" -Isaiah 52:7

Sister, when we are being called to be the hands and feet of Christ, we typically find ourselves being the hands more than the feet. Many of us have a servant's heart and our hands are always serving but, we are called to do more. We are called to strap on the shoes of the gospel and go out and tell others of the peace that Christ brings. If we are called to do this in the world, don't you think we are first called to do this in our own home. We are first called to tread on the foundation that God has set for our families, our marriage.

While the Roman soldiers wore shoes with hobnails to give them a better footing for battle. We are called to wear something slightly different. If we are going to "stand" against and "withstand" the enemy, we must make sure that our feet are strapped with the gospel of peace. We are to walk out the Gospel every single day. Because we have the peace of God that comes with the Gospel, we do not need to fear the attack of Satan or of men. We must be at peace with God and with each other if we are to defeat the Devil. (James 4:1-7)

The shoes also represent to us that we must be prepared each day to share the Gospel of peace with a lost world. The most victorious Christian is a witnessing Christian. The most victorious marriages are also a witness to the world of the Gospel. The number one purpose of your marriage has always been to represent the mystery of the Gospel. Your marriage is active and living and serves as a witness to the world of the love Christ has for His Church. We aren't perfect, we are broken people who live life in a broken world and we are called to do our very best with such conditions, but that's where the Gospel comes in.

If we wear the shoes of the Gospel, then we have the "beautiful feet" mentioned in Isaiah and Romans. Satan declared war, but you are an ambassador of peace within your own home first and then to the world. As a believer, you take the Gospel of peace wherever you go. Just as God reached out and found us and made us a promise, loved us, and continues to love us despite our faults, you are to do the same for your husband.

I don't know where you are in your marriage, if you're engaged, dreaming, newly married, decades in, full of love, loveless, full of memories, or memories not yet created. The good news is, that your marriage is so sacred to our Father that it is literally designed to reflect the Gospel of Jesus, a gospel of love. Whether broken or strong, happy or uninspiring, new or old, your marriage matters. You have a choice to be the good news every single day. Yes, the world needs you to be those beautiful feet on the mountain but so does your husband. Some wives are blessed to have husbands that are great men of God and some wives are hitting their knees praying for their husband's salvation. No matter where you are in your marriage, not matter what it looks like from the inside or outside, your marriage is cherished by the One who loves you most. Walk with footsteps that are readied with the gospel of peace.

Lord, I give You the glory that is due Your name for the work you have done here today. All blessing and honor and glory and power be to You. You are great and greatly to be praised. I bless You and magnify Your Holy name. Lord, in my worship and praise for You give me the wisdom to share your Gospel message. Place on my lips the words that the world needs to hear. In my marriage Lord, let it be a reflection of Your story of love and redemption. You are great, and You are a miracle worker. My marriage needs a miracle, it needs Your divine touch. Teach me Lord how to be ready with Your good news. Let me remember Your loving intentions for my marriage through hard times and the good. Lord, restore time that has been lost, and redeem words that have been said that do not reflect Your love. Magnify Your love for us through the representation of my marriage to others. Let your glorious ways be known on the earth and Your salvation among the nations. Thank you, Jesus. Amen

DAY 24: GUARD YOUR HEART

"*...with the breast plate of righteousness in place*"... -Ephesians 6:14

I'm going to be transparent here. For many years the word "righteous" put a bad taste in my mouth because of the context it is so often used in when describing someone who thinks they are better than all the rest and judges others based on their own goodness, "self-righteous". So, I struggled for years with understanding righteousness and what it meant concerning God. I have devoted prayer to asking for God to open up His Word to help me better understand what His righteousness means.

My study Bible took me on so many paths throughout scripture, it was quite a journey and created quite a reflection for me. Let me take you on the journey too.

"*Righteousness will be his belt and faithfulness the sash around his waist*" - Isaiah 11:5 referring to the coming Messiah.

"*Be dressed and ready for service and keep your lamps burning.*" - Luke 25:35 regarding the return of Christ.

"*Prepare your minds for action, be self-controlled; set your hopefully on the grace to be given to you when Jesus Chris is revealed.*" - 1 Peter 1:13

"*he put on righteousness as his breastplate.*" Isaiah 59:17 in reference again to the coming Messiah

"*Put on faith and love as a breastplate*" - 1 Thessalonians 5:8

I began to notice that all the references were in preparation and referred to putting on the armor. The breastplate literally guards the heart.

This piece of armor, made of metal plates or chains covered the body from the neck to waist, both front and back. It symbolizes the believer's righteousness in Christ as well as his righteous life in Christ.

"*God made him who had no sin to be sin for us, so that in him we might become the righteousness of God*" - 2 Corinthians 5:21

"*...and to put on the new self, created to be like God in true righteousness and holiness*" - Ephesians 4:24

Guard your heart.

For years I had a Sunday School teacher whom I admire as a godly wife and mother say at the closing of every class..."guard your heart and guard your marriage". You could call it part of her life song. She so pressed into us the importance of guarding both. The reason we must, at all times, protect our heart is because Satan will go straight for it and in turn his goal is to destroy our marriage.

Satan is the accuser, but he cannot accuse the believer who is living a godly life in the power of the Spirit. No, we aren't perfect in and of ourselves. We hope and strive to be more like Christ and walk this journey with Him. The life we live either fortifies us against Satan's attacks or makes it easier for him to defeat us. When we put on the breastplate of righteousness, we are not only guarding our hearts with the righteousness of Christ, but we are telling the world that we are going to live a life that fortifies us against Satan.

We stay away from the things of this world that Satan could use to attempt to destroy our lives and our marriage. We are careful about what our eyes see and our ears here. As children of the King, we must protect ourselves so that Satan cannot use our own actions against us. When Satan accuses the Christian, it is the righteousness of Christ that assures the believer of his salvation. But our positional righteousness in Christ, without practicing and walking out that righteousness daily, only gives Satan the opportunity to find a foothold to attack us. We must be diligent to "guard our hearts and guard our marriage" and not be tempted by the world.

Satan wants to wear you down and make your marriage feel loveless and miserable. Trust me, I walked out miserable for far too long many years ago. He wants to tarnish your marriage because doing so makes that picture of the gospel that your marriage represents appear tarnished too. He wants it to fail and be destroyed and the world has everything in it he needs to accomplish that goal. Guard your hearts and guard your marriage. Your Father gave you everything you need for unity in your marriage along with His desire for unity. The one thing Satan wants to do is divide and he will use what every unrighteousness in the world to do it. Put on that breastplate every single morning while His mercies are new. Decide for yourself and your husband that you will remain guarded.

Father, thank you. I cry out to you today as I put on my armor that You have bestowed. I claim victory over my marriage because I believe that the effective prayers of the righteous make Your heavenly power available to guard our hearts. Give me a steadfast spirit to be watchful of the enemy and his attempts to create a divide between myself and my husband. Lord, I yield to the Holy Spirit as he Helps me in my weakness and I plead the same for my husband. I pray the Spirit teaches us how to remain in your righteousness. Let all the days of our marriage and lives serve Your purposes here on earth. Release your power and glory upon our lives. I find the hope of our future in Your presence. Let the power of the Holy Spirit fill every area of my life with Your wisdom and courage. I know that I am called to wear this armor because of the battles we cannot see. Give me strength to withstand. In Christ Jesus name I pray these things. Amen.

DAY 25: TRUTH VS. THE LIAR

"Stand firm then with the belt of truth buckled around your waist". - Ephesians 6:14

The thing about a lie is, once it is told, it is sure that the truth will be revealed. Once the truth is revealed, trust is lost. The thing I have learned about the belt of truth is that it holds all of the rest of the armor in place. A life of integrity, with a clear conscience, can stop the enemy in his tracks without fear. Jesus instructs us to be ready and dressed in Luke 12:35. Prepare your minds! This is His instruction for us. Make sure your conscience is clear because to be fully dressed means the belt of truth is buckled and everything is firmly in place.

Satan is a liar.

"You belong to the father, the devil, and you want to carry your father's desire. He was a murdered from the beginning, not holding the truth, for there is no truth in him. When he lies, he speaks his native language, for he is a liar and the father of lies." -John 8:44

Straight from our Saviors lips he explains that you cannot be the daughter of the King and be the daughter of the devil. Who's your Daddy? You can make mistakes in your life, you will sin, you will live in the flesh, you will be human; our Heavenly Father knows this. What you need to know with all certainty is that you are His. You are the daughter of the King, the Lover of your soul, the One who created you, the One who blesses your spirit, and the One who will go to battle for you; need I go on? Know to Whom you belong. Remind yourself daily. It is essential to buckling on your armor and letting the belt of truth do its job.

The belt does hold all the parts together that we previously studied. There is a reason I gave them to you backwards. I wanted you to mentally strap each peace on each day and understand their purpose leading up to the truth. With the belt of truth holding it all in place you WILL BE victorious.

The belt also held the sword. The Sword of Truth the truth of God's Word goes together. Unless we practice the truth, we cannot use the Word of truth. Once a lie gets into the life of a believer, everything begins to fall apart.

King David lied. His lie and deceit grew and grew. He lied about Bathsheba and it was all downhill from there until he confessed and cleared his conscience. It was a brutal lie that cost lives. Psalms 32 and 51 tell of the price he paid.

Since we are fighting against our enemies in the spirit world, in the heavenly places, we need special equipment for offense and defense. God has provided it all, the full armor, the "whole armor" for us. It is important that we do not leave off one single part. Satan will look for the unguarded areas and he has an army following him. Do not let your guard down. Do not forget a piece. (Eph. 4:27) "Do not give the devil a foothold."

Paul commands his readers to put on the armor, take up the weapons, withstand Satan. We do it all by faith. We know that Christ has already conquered Satan. We know that the spiritual armor and weapons are available, by faith we accept what God gives us and go out to meet the foe. His fiery darts and lies cannot touch us. The day is evil, and the enemy is evil, but...

"if God is for us, who can be against us?" -Romans 8:31

"God is with her, she will not fail. He will help her at the break of day" -Psalm 46:5

Ladies, you are equipped. Before your feet hit the floor every morning, even if you have to set your alarm 5 mins earlier, lay in bed for just a bit and put your armor on. Empty your mind of the world, ask your Daddy God to capture your worldly thoughts and put on your armor. He created us to be warriors. We are in the army now! We are to strap on our armor and secure it with truth and study His word.

5 mins in the morning will set the entire tone of your day. Sometimes we do forget, and we are hurried. We start our day with a jolt and try to move

forward. We become of no use and feel beat down. Recently myself, I was trying to take care of a business matter that my husband needed me to handle. My entire morning was a mess, I was jolted from my bed as we had over slept. The kids missed the bus, I took them to school and tried to handle my day. It was a disaster for hours and my husband knew it, I made sure he did. I made a few calls and arrangements to meet with others later in the day so that I could go home and regroup. I had a "Goliath" to slay and I was doing it on my own. I gave myself a full hour to get it together and get my armor on and then asked for God's favor. What had taken me hours earlier (and gotten me nothing but an ill argument with my husband) was accomplished in less than 30 minutes with my armor on.

I cannot stress enough the difference that is made when you are prepared. Again, Jesus was very clear that we are to be dressed and ready (Luke 12:35) We are to prepare our minds. His words, not mine. If you do these things and still have a trying day, just imagine what it could have been like without your armor. The good news is, Christ can redeem it all and restore what is lost. Just ask. Just believe. Let's pray for ourselves and our husbands today.

Father God, I come to You today to thank You for Your mercies that are new every single morning. I praise You for Your sovereignty. Thank you for my whole armor, that every piece was considered and that everyone protects me. Lord, teach me to be faithful in putting my armor on, teach my husband also... Remind me when I'm missing a piece. Isaiah 40:31 tells me that if I wait for You Lord I will gain new strength and renewed power; that I will be lifted on wings and rise over the enemy like an eagle. From on high Lord, You will help me see where the Liar lurks. He cannot hide from You. You promise that I will run and not grow weary; that I will walk and not grow tired. Lord, help me. Help my unbelief Lord when my faith feels too small. Remind me whose I am every morning. I believe Your Word. Without you I can do nothing, not for myself, my husband, or my family. I need You and Your presence in my life. Lead me and guide me by Your Spirit. Show me Your ways. Lead me in the path of righteousness for Your name's sake. In Jesus Holy name, Amen..

DAY 26: VIRTOUS WOMAN

"Therefore, I urge you, (sisters), in view of God's mercy to offer your bodies as living sacrifices, holy and pleasing to God - this is your spiritual act of worship. Do not conform any longer to the pattern of this world but be transformed by the renewing of your mind. Then you will be able to test and approve what God's will is - his good, pleasing and perfect will." -Romans 12:1-2 (with additional comments)

Last night I had an awful dream. My dream was about my husband and me. At times it was weird and didn't make sense. My dream was that I drove my husband away. He was simply no longer interested in me and actually would much prefer someone different all together. When I woke up my heart was broken, my mind went directly to what I would do to keep my husband. It made me feel as though I would do anything to keep him and I wanted the "courting process" to start all over. I wanted to be delightful to be around and willing to put his needs before mine. I wanted to say..."Shove over world and leave us alone!"

Have you ever felt or even considered that the living sacrificial relationship you have with God also mirrors one you have with your husband? Have you ever felt the need or desire to lay it all down for him?

Now, I know my husband isn't leaving or looking, it was just a dream, but it does make me think about how willing I was in the beginning to please him. I would dress nice and talk sweeter...that was in the beginning. The beginning was many years ago. Should that change? Does it change? Do you think our husbands would appreciate if we went go back to those days? What if you set out to win your husband heart every single day? Just like God does for us.

When I think about what a godly and virtuous wife or woman would be like I immediately think on Proverbs 31:10-31

10Who can find a virtuous woman? for her price is far above rubies.
11The heart of her husband doth safely trust in her, so that he shall have no need of

spoil.
12She will do him good and not evil all the days of her life.
13She seeketh wool, and flax, and worketh willingly with her hands.
14She is like the merchants' ships; she bringeth her food from afar.
15She riseth also while it is yet night, and giveth meat to her household, and a portion to her maidens.
16She considereth a field, and buyeth it: with the fruit of her hands she planteth a vineyard.
17She girdeth her loins with strength, and strengtheneth her arms.
18She perceiveth that her merchandise is good: her candle goeth not out by night.
19She layeth her hands to the spindle, and her hands hold the distaff.
20She stretcheth out her hand to the poor; yea, she reacheth forth her hands to the needy.
21She is not afraid of the snow for her household: for all her household are clothed with scarlet.
22She maketh herself coverings of tapestry; her clothing is silk and purple.
23Her husband is known in the gates when he sitteth among the elders of the land.
24She maketh fine linen, and selleth it; and delivereth girdles unto the merchant.
25Strength and honour are her clothing; and she shall rejoice in time to come.
26She openeth her mouth with wisdom; and in her tongue is the law of kindness.
27She looketh well to the ways of her household, and eateth not the bread of idleness.
28Her children arise up, and call her blessed; her husband also, and he praiseth her.
29Many daughters have done virtuously, but thou excellest them all.
30Favour is deceitful, and beauty is vain: but a woman that feareth the LORD, she shall be praised.
31Give her of the fruit of her hands; and let her own works praise her in the gates.

Maybe we should read through those again....

The virtuous woman brings her husband pride, she is not lazy, she does good by her husband and puts much thought and effort into her responsibilities, every one of them. Her words are thought out, she is kind, she is not vain, and she is always prepared. When I personally read through all these things that describe the virtuous woman, I make a mental list of all the things I am not.

There was a time when I read through these and thought, I'm not doing too bad. I think I might work on one of these I'm not doing well though.

Proverbs 31:15 was the one I chose. Which one would you choose? I definitely have the desire to take care of my family and it would not hurt me at all to wake up a little before them each morning and get it together. I could spend time in prayer, put on my armor, and adjust my attitude. So many little things can be accomplished by getting ahead of my family during the day. I'm not the best at it but my alarm goes off every morning before my husbands. That was my desire. Yours may be totally different.

Why is this all important to consider?

It would not have been placed in God's Holy Word if it was not important. We surely do not want our husbands studying on these things for us. Instead, have a talk with God about the things you can do better or work on. Reflect on your marriage in the beginning, in the "courting" or "honeymoon" stages when your best foot was put forward and think of one thing that you did then for your husband that you no longer do that he might still appreciate. If he appreciated the efforts then, he will appreciate them now.

The Bible has so much to say about the body. God cares about your body because He dwells within it. If you want to know what God has in store for you, what His will is for your marriage, offer your body to Him as a living sacrifice. Do all you can to present it as the best possible self you can. Take care of yourself, get rest and sleep, eat well, exercise, avoid anything that may compromise your health. Study His Word, guard your tongue, protect your eyes and ears from what you see and hear. Not only do you deserve to take care of yourself, but God expects you to take care of you. If you aren't taking care of yourself, how can you possibly give your marriage, husband, or family the care it needs.

The relationship of the believer to Jesus Christ is as the relationship of husband and wife. You share, you belong, you are one; emotionally physically, mentally, spiritually one. Yes, you are two separate creations of God, but He has called you to be one.

Father, I want to know You more intimately. I give my life to You; my physical body was created to worship You and You perfectly dwell within me. Spirit teach me to take better care of myself, show me what God says is important for me, make His will for my life evident. I want to glorify Your name in all that I do and say. Keep my mind alert, train me up as a child of Yours. Lord, I ask that you continue to put a divide between myself and the world. The world does to offer me a thing that is of value to You. Only Your goodness and grace that meets my every need is acceptable. Show me Lord where there needs to be pruning in my life, show me where I can flourish for your Kingdom. Give me an eternal perspective so that I can see farther. I know You never reveal the full picture of our purpose but step by step You guide, guide me. I give you my life and my body so that I may serve and be Your hands and feet in this world that does **not** *know You. Thank you, Lord, for promises. Thank you, Lord, for reminding me that I am Yours. In Jesus Holy Name, Amen.*

DAY 27: OPEN & SHUT

"All Scripture is inspired by God and is profitable for teaching, for rebuking, for correcting, for training in righteousness, so that the man of God may be complete, equipped for EVERY good work." - 2 Timothy 3:16-17, emphasis added

That also includes His guidance for His children. He will do whatever is possible to help you know His will for your marriage. It is essential, however, that you watch for His hand in your life so that you are able to discern the circumstances for what they are. He will create them as He opens and shuts doors, just let God be God.

"Call me and I will answer you and tell you great and unsearchable things you do not know." -Jeremiah 3:33

Sometimes it feels like you aren't sure what doors to walk through. As husband and wife, that is when it becomes very important to pray together. God has never failed us when we ask Him to reveal His will. Sometimes He shuts other doors, sometimes He makes the path straight, sometimes He shines a light for us. Watch for His favor and use what He gave you. He gave you eyes to see and ears to hear.

His Word also speaks. When you begin to see His Word as a living, life breathing Book you will begin to stop reading as mere stories and black and white words. Before even opening His Word, ask for guidance like He offers in Jeremiah 33:3 and His Word will change how you read and what you receive. It will begin to speak to you in the places that need filling up with Him. He may guide you, but He will be clear in His guidance. He may never give you the full picture but being obedient to His will and keeping an eternal perspective of your marriage will change you and guide you.

Read Acts 16:6-12. Paul and Timothy were actually forbidden by the Holy Spirit to go to Asia. Their course instead was straight to Macedonia, led by the prompting of the Holy Spirit. One door closed and another opened. God has inherently equipped you with what it takes to know His will.

Asking for the Holy Spirit for His help in discernment can be the key to making sure the doors opened are wide. Prayer opens them wide just like the gates of heaven.

In 2011, around the first week of September, just after Labor Day; my husband lost his job. The job he'd had for 6 years. I was probably the only woman whose husband had lost his job in that tanked economy and was happy about it. Number one, I knew the job was slowly killing him and number two our marriage had been suffering. A week before he was given the "pink slip", we'd had the biggest fight of our marriage. One that made me call it quits. I was done. My husband was completely miserable, and he was making all of us miserable. I knew the instant that I saw him when he walked through the door and started to hand me his release papers that it was God. Sure, circumstances may have led up to that day but if it had not been for God stepping in I am not sure I would have had the strength to keep trying. Because I knew that this was a God thing, I knew that He was in control of our lives and was working on something big. In the meantime, my husband and I had more time to study God's Holy Word and to spend more time with our Father. We are leaning on Him and seeking out His Will for us. Sometimes, when things get so bad that we feel we cannot go any further, God steps in and takes over.

Can you look back on any situation in your life, that at the time you thought was devastating, and now you see how God used that circumstance to give you better than you ever imagined? Have you ever seen Him take pain and hurt and turn it into something healing and beautiful?

There is a time for everything, a season for every activity under the heaven. A time to be born and a time to die, a time to plant and a time to uproot, a time to kill and a time to heal, a time to tear down and a time to build, a time to weep and a time to laugh, a time to more and a time to dance... - Ecclesiastes 3:1-8

Sometimes, it's just time to walk through another door.

Looking back, years later, I definitely see that our Father had better things in store for us. It was one of the best door closings of our lives. We definitely wanted to be where He needed us to be and where we would find Him working. I have learned since, in the face of tragedies and disappointments to say immediately; "Well, God's got something better for us." He has been very faithful on this matter of door closing. The doors that opened have led us far beyond our expectations and imaginations.

Watch Him work. You've read your Bible, you've asked for guidance, you've prayed diligently for His help, now watch Him work. When your marriage goals and desires line up with His will for you, amazing works begin to happen that can only be explained by Him. As our marriage is a reflection of the Gospel so is the Great Commission in application as well. Your marriage is a reflection of what God can do for others.

Lord Father, I will hope in You. I will live to serve you with gladness and live righteously. I will praise Your holy name forever. I partake of Your mercies that are new every morning. Your love for me never fails, and Your mercy endures. Lord, I ask that You cut off and close doors to the things in my life that are preventing me to walk in you will. Lord, I ask that you cut off and close all doors for my husband if anything is preventing him from walking in Your will. I am blessed because I put my trust in You. I thank You, Lord that your heart is for my marriage and I will continually bless You and praise You. Lord, I ask you today to make our path clear as husband and wife. Show us with all certainty the doors we should walk through. Your Word is true. Lord I thank you that with Your mighty hand you close doors. Just like closing the door to the ark, You protected your creation from the Great Flood. Lord, protect my marriage. In Jesus Holy name, Amen.

DAY 28: LOVE, SWEET LOVE

"For I know the plans I have for you" declares the Lord, "plans to prosper you and not to harm you, plans to give you a hope and a future" -Jeremiah 29:11

I can't read that verse and not immediately want to jump to this one.

"For you created my inmost being; you knit me together in my mother's womb. I praise you because I am fearfully and wonderfully made; your works are wonderful, I know that full well. My frame was not hidden from you when I was made in the secret place. When I was woven together in the depths of the earth, your eyes saw my unformed body. All the days ordained for me were written in your book before one of them came to be." - Psalm 139:13-16

Give Him your heart. You can trust Him with it, He made it. He made you special and you were chosen to be here in this moment at this time. You are so very special to Him that you were carefully, thoughtfully, fearfully created, crafted, and designed by God your Father. Before He even created this world, He had a plan for you. You are no accident, no afterthought. He didn't make you up as He went along. He created you and willed you into this life for a purpose. He chose your parents and wove you together in the womb. He knew where you would be born among your generations before you and what order you were to be born. He even planned and chose for you your spiritual heritage. Some parts you may not consider beautiful, but He does. Some parts you see as He does, gorgeous. You're a perfect creation with the desire to seek out your Father's love. He gave you everything you need to overcome everything that needs over coming, even your heritage if needed.

In a previous day's devotion, I asked the question: If God made you to be the perfect wife to your husband, do you believe that you are her?

There are some days when that answers feels like a firm and solid "no". There are days when you may want to shout "absolutely". Hopefully, the "no" days are very few. There was a time in our marriage when the "no" days outweighed the "absolutely" days. Now, there is no question, even on our hardest days my answer is always "absolutely". God has invested so much in you and your marriage that you may not even see or know. You may be two imperfect people that He created perfectly, people the world has broken and sinned against, but He created you BOTH exactly as you should be. You then chose each other to walk through this life journey together and He will bless it.

An incredible amount of effort and time was used to design you. Our Father focused and made you one of a kind. He did not take the safe route and just start making copies of people. No, He took His time and did it right when He made you. He did the same thing for your husband. He planned and thought about you so extensively, far beyond the age of this earth. He knew your soul before it was placed in His earthly creation. He smiles when He looks at you and He smiles when He looks at you and your husband together. He is waiting and watching for you both to acknowledge His presence and all He has to offer you in this life.

The world needs the two of you to remain faithful in your marriage and to each other. The world needs you. You are both bringing something special that no other couple of individuals in the world can bring. You each have gifts, that when combined, have the power to change people's thinking about what marriage should look like. Other people you know, need to see what God has done. God gave you the power to show the world what is possible when it comes to marriage.

We don't know what God's plan is. We don't know what our future chapters look like or even how long He has written them, our days are ordained. During that time, God does not promise that things won't get hard or painful. He doesn't promise that we will have worry free days until we take our last breath but what He does promise is, we can run to Him. He promises that He can turn the pain and hard stuff into beauty and dancing. His power and promises are all tied together with the love that He has for you. You and your husband were both created to be loved by Him, to seek His love, and to desire that relationship.

We are to not just know there is a God or believe that Jesus walked on this Earth. We should also desire to have a relationship with Him that is intimate. The intimacy was designed from the very beginning and when He released you into this world He wanted nothing more than you to turn back to Him and embrace His love. Graft into Him. Jesus said *"I am the true vine, and my Father is the Gardener..."* -John 15:1 If we will remain in Jesus, Jesus will remain in us and God our Father Gardener will take care of the rest. He will surround us with beauty and pull the weeds for us. He will help us to bear fruit and trim away the things in our life that prevent us from being fruitful.

Your marriage was written into His chapters. As the Author and Perfecter of our lives you can trust that the life He has for You was designed for something more beautiful than you can imagine. He will continue to place in your life, everything you need to strengthen your marriage.

Lord, I present myself and my marriage to You. I desire to draw nearer to You with my entire heart. I give myself back to You. I want to be holy and acceptable to You. The world changed me, and its influence does little good. My life is in Your hands today, just like it was the day You first thought of me until the moment You created me. I give You my heart and all of the pains and disappointments. Create in me, Daddy God, a clean heart, and renew in me a steadfast spirit. Lord take my marriage and transform it into Your image of marriage. Make my husband and I like You. Show us why You created us. I believe Your Word. You are the vine and I am the branch. I will abide and remain in You all of the days you have ordained in my life. Without You I can do nothing. I need You and Your presence at all times. Lead us and guide us by Your Spirit. We want to have the fruit that remains and is waiting for us. We desire and ask for godly character a we abide in You. Show us Your ways. Lead us down the path of righteousness for Your name's sake. In Your name Jesus I pray, Amen.

.

DAY 29: SLOW TO ANGER

"Better a patient man, than a warrior, a man who controls his temper than who takes a city" -Proverbs16:32

We recently walked through what it means to put on our full armor and be ready for battle. We are in the army of God and are called to do those things but sometimes it is all for not, if we let our temper get the better of us.

I read something once that said, "Love is hard to offend and quick to forgive." If our love wasn't quick to forgive, my husband and I would not have been together for these last 25 plus years. There are days when I wonder if this is true in our relationship though.

I remember a time when my husband came home from a long day at work and barely said two words when he walked in the door, he wouldn't answer my question until he was ready and then made a comment that he knew would rub me the wrong way before going out the door. It wasn't that he was doing it on purpose to be mean, he just didn't withhold his frustrations and I was the one that happened to be in the way. He had something bothering him and so did I. However, I couldn't even react to his snarky comment except to thrust my mop down in the water so hard the water flew of my bucket. Only to think to myself..."why'd I do that, now I have to clean it up." [sigh] It immediately made me think of how we can spill so much over onto others when we are shaken, what do we spill over? Whatever we are full of.

I know it was silly, but I anger easily sometimes. It makes me want to scream in frustration that I lack so little self-control but screaming probably would not look much like self-control either. In reality, I know I need to do better. I need to not throw a ridiculous tantrum and try to practice more patience and kindness.

"...the compassionate and gracious God, slow to anger, abounding in love and

faithfulness." -Exodus 34:6

"The Lord is slow to anger, abounding in love and forgiving sin and rebellion..." - Numbers 14:18

"...But you are a forgiving God, gracious and compassionate, slow to anger and abounding in love." - Nehemiah 9:17

"But you, O Lord, are a compassionate and gracious God, slow to anger, abounding in love and faithfulness." - Psalm 86:15

"I knew that you are a gracious and compassionate God, slow to anger and abounding in love, a God who relents from sending calamity." - Jonah 4:2

I don't know about you, but I want to be known in this life for something, I want it to be that I am compassionate and gracious, slow to anger, and abounding in love. These verses strike a chord with me every single time a read them.

Slow to anger...slow to anger...that is something I don't feel I naturally come by. My husband has known me a long time and certainly knows which button to push if he wanted to get a rise. He knows what rubs me the wrong way and how to irritate me and I know I'm not alone. As a "loving wife", I should be gentle and calm, cheerful and self-controlled. I cannot be these things part of the time. I must be these things all of the time, right? If it doesn't anger God, it shouldn't anger me because ultimately my reaction is probably what would have made God mad and not the fact that my husband didn't pick up his own laundry or call when he was going to be late. My emotional self-control would do much more for my marriage than a romantic weekend getaway ever could (although, that would be nice).

We need to learn to quickly forgive and forget at a much faster rate. We need to keep our day and our lives better balanced and pace ourselves so that we do not feel the stress of being a wife and/or a mom all of the time. We need to be more grateful for the life and love that we have. How do we do that exactly?

Breathe! We just need to breathe. Standing still, closing my eyes for a second while chaos tries to overwhelm me, and breathe. Isn't that what God commands of us. Be still and know. Be still. Breathe. Then we can thank Him for just being Him. For being the calm in our storm and our strength. Thank Him, praise Him. Just speak His praise out loud. "Thank you, Lord. Thank you, Jesus." Oh, how those words take you from a place of less to a place of more; from a place with less hope to a place full of hope. You know that in your thankfulness, that you have allowed God to pour out on your life, everything you need, in His fullness. He will fill you up. So that when you are shaken, you splash Him everywhere. There will be no mess to clean up. Let Him fill you. So, now...you can let it go. Let go of the anger, let go of the frustration, let go of the weight that you just tried to pick up and carry. He never intended for you to carry that.

Next time you find yourself with your head in your hands and you aren't feeling His peace, do this. Take note. Write down exactly how you are feeling at that very moment. Then, praise God. Just jot down or say out loud a truth about God. (i.e., "Lord, thank You for...") After a moment of praise, take note. Write down how you feel after your praise. I promise you, He will take you from a moment of feeling less to a feeling as though He is about to do something amazing, something more.

The reason we get so angry is simply because things aren't going the way we want them to go. We were not in complete control of the circumstance. It cannot be that hard to start letting God handle it and trusting that that He has our best interest at heart. Even if things aren't going our way, being slow to anger, is a virtue that can save a marriage.

Father, I thank You that You have mercy and grace in Your heart for me. I will continually bless and praise You. Your Word is true. Your love never fails, and Your mercies endure forever. I am blessed that you are slow to anger and let love abound. I can put my trust in You because my hope, confidence, and expectation are in You. I will not let my anger cut off my hope and blessings a day more. Holy Spirit, be my guide, rain down on me the fruit of Your Spirit that gives me the patience and long-suffering that I need. It is a fruit that you can bestow so that I can continually hope in You. Your heart is for me and I know that You will not withhold from me these things that I ask. These are the ways in which I can become more like Jesus and You give them freely. Teach me to breathe and rejoice, breathe and rejoice. Thank you, Lord, for all You have done, are doing now, and about to do in my marriage. My husband and I need Your presence Lord and Your Peace. Thank you, Father. In Jesus Holy and Mighty Name. Amen..

DAY 30: ANOINTED MARRIAGE

There are so many things that God has unraveled for me over the last few years, just like pulling the string on a sweater, it unravels faster and faster until what was there before needs to be knitted back together entirely. So many things I never understood after being in church my entire life were overwhelming me. The Holy Spirit knows this about me. Recently I began to experience the Spirit as He was intended to be. As I sit here with my essential oil diffuser misting into the air it reminds me of how I viewed the spirit for almost 35 years of my life. As a mist that comes and hovers and can be felt but there was nothing more for me.

A few years ago, I sat in our church sanctuary after a service with my heart pounding. I kept saying to myself "there's something more." The journey of getting to know the Holy Spirit like I never had is definitely a story for another day. There are so many beautiful words in the Bible that started to come alive for me as I began studying God's Word with a fresh assurance. One of the words I have been seeking more guidance on is the word "anointing". I found that in my spiritual dry spells is when I needed His anointing to flood my spirit and awaken in me a desire to fully press into the Father.

How do we get to the oil (or anointing) to soothe a dry spell? The olive tree tells us how.

First, the tree itself must be rooted in the right soil, just as we must be rooted in the Word of God and the tree will grow, mature and blossom producing fruit. In biblical times, as well as today, the very best fruit is at the top, it is not the fruit that has already dropped. It is the fruit that must be *shaken* from the tree. When the tree is shaken, the olives fall from the tree and must be caught gently before hitting the ground, gathered together and washed. Then the fruit must be pressed to release the oil, it must be broken so that the pure oil will flow. The pulp is collected and used again to extract the most precious oil. It is a time-consuming process that requires tremendous pressure.

It just so happens, about a week ago, I watched short film on how olive oil is made, and it was a very beautiful process to watch.

"Christ, the sinless One, required no preparation for receiving the anointing oil, a symbol of the Holy Spirit" -Hebrews 1:9

"But you have an anointing from the Holy One and all of you know the truth."- 1 John 2:20

"As for you, the anointing you received from him remains in you, and you do not need anyone to teach you. But as his anointing teaches you about all things and as that anointing is real, not counterfeit - just as it has taught you, remain in him." - 1 John 2:27

"God, your God, has set your above your companions by anointing you with the oil of joy" -Hebrews 1:9

"God gives the Spirit without limit" -John 3:34

The anointing oil, being representative of the Spirit of God, is without limit.

Sometimes we feel dry (in our marriage or relationship with Christ), we feel like God is nowhere around. Sometimes we feel like we are not anointed at all. For any number of reasons or any amount of time a marriage can go through a dry spell. When this happens, just remember the olive tree. Olive oil was a staple of the diet in Biblical times. Deuteronomy 8:8 talks about God delivering the children of Israel into a land of milk, honey, wheat, and olive oil (among other things). God's people went through a very rough dry spell in their desert of testing. God delivered them. Olive oil was also used as medicine in Luke 10:34 by the Samaritan. Olive oil was used as lamp fuel (for light) and is the process of purification is described in Lev. 24: 1-2. Finally, olive oil was used for anointing in religious offerings and rituals as representing the pouring out of God's Spirit.

Just the imagery used of a tree being shaken made me hold my breath. Aren't we all shaken? Aren't we sitting here reading this and thinking of all the ways our marriage has been shaken? To have ever gotten to the point of being shaken, means that your marriage is grounded, it is rooted in something good, has matured and has produced fruit, otherwise, you would not be here at this very moment reading this in an effort to do something good for your marriage. Has your marriage felt dry? That's what the oil is for? How are we going to get that oil?

The oil as described started with the shaking of the tree, some stress has to be applied to force that tree to let go of the fruits it is holding on to in order to move forward in extracting the oil. What are you holding on too? Are you bitter? Are you angry? Is the love in your marriage drying up? Is there something or someone weaseling its way into your marriage to separate you from your husband physically or emotionally? Are you ready to let go of the things in your life that you are holding on to so that you can move forward?

Now, remember, when you are shaken, and you let go of these things, God is there to catch you when you fall. He is going to gather up all of the things that have been growing in your life and your marriage and He is going to sort them for you. He's going to keep the good and throw out the bad and He is going to use the good, healthy, mature, pure and perfect fruits of your marriage. What God is going to do with those good fruits is wash them, just as Jesus washed us of our sins, God is going to wash your fruits and get them ready. Once your marriage has been shaken, there will be a calm, a tranquility before God brings you through the press. I don't know what your "press" is going to be, but God is going to put the pressure on so that you will trust Him, lean on Him, call on Him and give your marriage to Him. After your marriage has been pressed through, what will come out of it is the purest anointing oil to heal your marriage that God could possibly ever give.

This beautiful anointing is coming to your marriage, but you have to be ready for the shaking and the pressing. As God presses you, you press into Him. Seek His guidance through His Word and through prayer.

Father, oh how I need You to pour Your Spirit out onto me. Lord, fill me completely with your Spirit from head to toe so that I can move forward completely filled by You. Press out of me what is not of You so that there is room for you to fill me up. Remove my impurities and prepare my marriage for any shaking and sifting it may need. Lord, I ask you to remove anything from my marriage that doesn't belong, open my eyes to see what You see. Take our good fruits and press them as we press into You. Lord, shake us so that the world cannot. I want You to use our good fruits rather than have the world trample on them. We trust you with our shaking and that you will catch all that falls away and use it for good. I thank You, Lord, that You are not like man. You are a God of integrity. Your words are an anchor for my soul and You are my refuge. I run to You and I am safe. Sift me Lord, sift my marriage. I will wait for You and the fulfillment of Your words. In Jesus Holy Name, Amen.

DAY 31: ADOPTED

Ladies, we are adopted. We are daughters of a Mighty King and He has so much to teach us. The next 10 days are dedicated to that relationship with God: Father God, Jesus, and the Holy Spirit. I want to unravel for you ideals, religion, and lies. I pray that the next 10 days are the most powerful words you will read in this study. This study is a tool; it's a supplement to the Bible. We are going to dive into His open and living Word and pray for transformation as wives. We will transform our thinking and know that He is the One who orchestrates the parts of our marriage that is at peace and full of love. He walks us through the hard times and stands near us through every fight and ill word. He's just waiting for us to ask for help, seek forgiveness, give forgiveness, ask for wisdom, and favor. He wants us to realize on the very deepest level, our souls, that we are His daughters and He expects us to walk this life as such.

As I prepared for this day's devotion I found myself circling my living room in prayer with arms open wide as if surrounding myself with His presence. Praying for Spirit wisdom and for Him to teach me what I needed to know most. See, we all fall short. We will often find ourselves being the wives we weren't called to be and with a heavy shame I asked for forgiveness for the way I had treated my husband previously. It is hard living with another person and walking this walk. I wanted to open up some scripture for you, like God has opened it for me. Let's visit Matthew 5 together.

You are the salt of the earth, but if salt has lost its taste, how shall its saltiness be restored? It is no longer good for anything (or anyone) except to be thrown out and trampled under people's feet. YOU are the light of the world. A city set on a hill cannot be hidden. Nor do people light a lamp and put it under a basket, but on a stand, and it gives light to all in the house. In the same way, let YOUR light shine before others, so that they may see your good works and give glory to your Father in heaven. - Matthew 5:13-15 (emphasis added)

The Lord speaks to us in different ways; for me, He speaks in vision and images. When I read this scripture, I have many images. You are a light. Picture it, a city on a hill, lit by light from within for all to see. I think about the little song I sing to my daughter "This Little Light of Mine." Her favorite part is when we sing "Hide it under a bushel...NO! I'm gonna let it shine." Ladies, we sing these words into our babies, but the Lord is singing it into us. We would never want to diminish our children's little lights. We want them to shine so bright and our Father wants the same for us. He wants others to see us and our lights. Our lights from within are completely fueled by His love for us and the relationship He desires to have with us. Jesus did not unveil the Father for us to stay hidden. The veil was torn.

We are called to bring the light to others and especially our husbands. The one person in the entire world the Lord wanted you to cling to and spend your life with deserves your light. He deserves to see your light shine from within and we have got to stop putting "bushels or baskets" over it. We are called to put our light on a lampstand. To stand and be still and to just shine. We don't need to even run around spreading our light, the light attracts, we need only be still.

When we hide our light, we diminish our influence to bring God right into our marriage. Our marriage benefits when we build our relationship with God. As our fuel, our anointing oil, our flames shine brighter and brighter as that strong connection is built. We are empowered to live the way Jesus intended us to live. In His glory, by the Gospel, we have an unbreakable connection that will never fail us in our moments of deepest testing.

We cannot fail to pursue a personal relationship with God, we can no longer sit on the side lines and watch the world influence our husbands or our families. We must seek a relationship with God. What does that mean? It wasn't until the last several years, that the Lord truly started exposing for me the lies in my life and where they started. Sadly, many of my influences came from religious encounters as a child. They were so deeply woven into my being that I had no idea they could even be unraveled. I asked for wisdom and I received it.

Do not be conformed to this world, but be transformed by the renewal of your mind, that by testing you may discern what is the will of God, what is good and acceptable and perfect. - Romans 12:2

In order to build the relationship I needed to with God I had to transform my thoughts and renew my mind. Have you ever noticed that it seems like "new Christians" have a better grasp for what Christ has done for us than many other people we know? I have, and it blows me away. I was saved as a young child and I thank God over and over for that grace in my life. However, I knew that I was missing something. There was an evening at church when I didn't want to leave. I kept telling my husband "I know I'm saved, I love Jesus but I'm missing something." I was. I was missing so much. Shortly after praying for God to reveal to me what I was missing I picked up a book a friend had written about the power of the Holy Spirit. The first words that jumped off the page went something like "do you feel like you're missing something". I did not put that book down.

I was missing a connection with the Spirit. The Spirit is available to us all, but I had no clear understanding of what He was in my life. I saw the Holy Spirit as a mist or unclear substance and believed the lie that He was not always available to me. I believed that the Holy Spirit was a spiritual substance and not a Person desiring a very intimate relationship with me. I have a feeling, you may be reading this and say..."me too." The next 10 days, I'm going to introduce God to you as a whole. I want to introduce you to the Spirit as He has been introduced to me. I want you to experience the life changing, marriage changing, belief changing, wisdom growing, Helper that we have waiting for our call.

God communicates with each of us in unique ways. I want to help you experience Him in a way that allows an open line of communication so that you can see and feel His presence in your life. I don't tread lightly here, this is the most impactful part of healing your marriage, saving your marriage, restoring your marriage, redeeming your marriage, and delivering your marriage. If this is what you desire, then the next steps are going to change you, transform your mind, unravel wrong thinking, and renew your mind in the truths that God has for your marriage. It all starts with YOU and your relationship with Father God, Jesus, and the Holy Spirit.

Until your mind is renewed, you will struggle with mentalities that are in opposition of what God wants you to experience in this life journey with your husband. We are going to confront these mentalities head on with the armor that God has given us, with the Fruits of the Spirit that He has sown into us. It's going to feel like someone pulled a string and you started spinning like a top. You're going to spin and spin and spin and in the midst of it all you will find that your light grows brighter and brighter. The whole world is going to see what God can do in a marriage. It's not my job to save your marriage. It's not. It's my job to show you what is possible. Pray with me.

Father God, I come to You asking that You reveal Yourself to me. I ask that You help me sense, see, and hear You. Help me to discern the lies the world has impressed upon me that hinder a personal relationship with You. Lord, I ask that You reveal Your Holy Spirit to me in such a way that I know without a doubt that His presence is within Me. I need Your Help. My Helper is waiting, and I ask that You help me build a stronger connection with You. Lord, I ask that You place in my heart a deep desire to know You. Help me believe during my unbelief that You are for me, Father. Reveal Your love and truth. I have a desire to know Jesus, my Savior, on a deeper more personal level. A level deeper than I know, one that my soul desires. Lord I hand You my life, I surrender my life to You. Show me new and glorious things, renew my mind, transform my heart, and remove ungodly mindsets. Lord, bless my husband through this. Help me show Him the relationship He can have with You. Thank you, Lord, that You have given me the armor I need to protect myself during this time of fresh renewing. In Jesus' sweet and Holy name, I pray. Amen

DAY 32: A FRIEND

So many of our relationships in our life, including our marriage, directly impact our relationship with Jesus. Instead of allowing Him to be our gold standard we allow our past relationships to tell us how Jesus feels about us.

Greater love has no other than this, that someone lay down his life for his friends. - John 15:13

Jesus fills many roles for us during our life and no one role is more important than the other. What I want to focus on today for you is His friendship and love for us. Jesus wants to help release us of mindsets that are not true of Him or of ourselves. He wants to give us complete and total healing from the lies we have attached to Him and to ourselves so that where healing needs to happen in our relationships, especially with our husbands, it becomes possible.

For I am sure that neither death nor life, nor angels, nor rulers, nor things present nor things to come, nor powers, nor height nor depth, nor anything else in all creation, will be able to separate us from eh love of God in Christ Jesus our Lord - Romans 8:38-39

Nothing can keep us from Him. We have the power through Him to reveal and remove all that we attached to our relationship to Him that is false. He is waiting for you, friend. Once, we lift these lies we will experience Him in ways that change our relationships with those we love and encounter daily. Jesus was, is, and forever will be God (John 1:1-14) He came to be with us, so we could experience Him even today. He can relate to any and all situations we are faced with because he experienced a physical existence with us. He left with us a relationship with Him that means we have a relationship with the Father too. He represents the greatest friendship and love we can ever have. We get to experience Him in every moment of our life. He gave us the ultimate gift, redemption through His sacrifice of stepping down from His Throne to join us, to the gift of His death, and the glory of rising again as Conqueror. Yes, that guy...He is our Friend.

All over the world, every day, relationships are formed and broken; we base them all on how we are treated and how we feel. Not Jesus, He chooses us regardless of whether we like Him or not. He chose us despite how we treat or think of Him. He does this so that it is up to us if we accept or reject Him as friend. Knowing this, how do you now think of your marriage?

Behold I stand at the door and knock. If anyone hears My voice and opens the door, I will come in to him and eat with him, and he with Me. -Revelation 3:20

Once we accept His gift of the cross, we are forever marked by His love. We get to experience this life with Him and He wants to experience it with you. The image of Jesus sitting with me and tasting this life with me blows me away. The Bible tells us that He is not only a friend but also like a big Brother.

Therefore, He had to be made like His brothers in every respect, so that He m might become a merciful and faithful high priest in the service of God, to make propitiation for the sins of the people. - Hebrews 2:17

King Jesus is our friend, even better than a brother (Proverbs 18:24). As a "younger sibling" of Jesus we can access all that He owns. As children of God we become co-heirs of His Kingdom. We can BOLDY go before the Throne of Grace (Her 4:6) because we belong there. We are not simply visitors. While we are there Jesus intercedes on our behalf continuously. He is our Savior, Friend, and Mediator at all times. Our past relationships create in us an expectation of Jesus. It is time to reverse this mindset and let our relationship with Jesus create an expectation of all past and future earthly relationships. We can no longer let the world color the way we see Jesus. We need to let Jesus color the way we see the world.

Forgiveness is one of the most powerful tools that we have. It is a powerful weapon against the enemy. Unforgiveness chains us to moments in our past that we are not to carry with us and we always hold the key that will release us from those chains, forgiveness. Our guilt and shame are roadblocks to healing and strain our relationship with Christ. Jesus imparts forgiveness on us and we must do the same for others. He wants to take the responsibility so that we can let go and experience freedom.

Any lies that the enemy uses to deceive us regarding our relationship with our husband can cause distance between us and Jesus. It is time, that we ask Jesus to relate to us each in person on a personal level. It is rewarding to watch Jesus replace His Truth in the areas of pain within our marriage or any area of our life. Jesus heals hurts, removes lies and imparts truth. That's what He does for us. We are going ask our Friend for help. We have so much that needs healing.

In prayer today, we are going to ask Jesus to reveal any lies about our relationship with Him that may be affecting our relationship with our husband. We are going to let Jesus expose those lies and where they started. We are going to ask Him to reveal Himself and to help us forgive anyone who taught us this lie. He will remove ungodly mindsets and replace them with truth. It's time to let our Friend, our Savior, heal any brokenness in our marriage that is a direct result of relationship with Him.

For myself, Jesus continues to reveal my spirit of rejection. He heals those moments for me when I experienced them and shows me how to forgive. My spirit and even fear of rejection has caused strains in my marriage, believing that one day I may not be the bride to my husband that he wants or deserves often made me want to go ahead and throw in the towel. Jesus broke those chains for me one by one. Whatever lie your chains have attached you to, will be broken. He promises to do so.

Jesus, I come to You today to thank You for being a Friend to me. Lord, I ask that You reveal to me a lie that has been impressed upon me about You or myself. Show me, Jesus, where this lie was first placed and reveal to me how that made You feel during that moment. I want to feel Your presence during the memory so that I will know how to forgive. I want to see my experience through Your eyes. I ask that You unchain me from the lie and replace that mindset with one of truth. Forgive me Jesus for not running to you before now and believing anything other than Your truth. Cast out all of the ungodly thoughts that I have that tarnish my relationship with You and in turn have tarnished my relationship with my husband. Help me to see how You love me. Help me to transfer this forgiveness and love to my husband. Lord Jesus, help me to forgive always. In Your Precious Name, Amen.

DAY 33: YOUR DADDY GOD

Being raised in church, for me, did not equal an automatic relationship with God as a whole. Walking into the throne room in prayer before the Father was not something I understood and will probably not understand in its fullness until I am in His presence in Heaven. However, it is a place that Jesus has escorted me into many times in my life. When I thought of Father God, many feelings began to rise up in me. I knew when I started my marriage study I would need to enter His presence daily and that felt almost impossible to imagine because of the shame I wore like a garment. However, with Jesus, I found where I belonged, right in my Daddy God's arms.

Daddy God is a description I like to use, that a friend shared with me, to help me understand His love for us.

I want to walk you through scripture because, I can tell you about my life long building relationship experience or you can experience Him yourself through His Word. First, let's talk about Jesus, our friend. He's going to introduce us to His Father. Jesus has so much love and honor for Him, we can't help but want to know His Daddy too.

...You are my Son; today I have become your Father. -Psalm 2:7

He will call out to me, 'You are my Father, my God, the Rock my Savior - Psalm 89:26

I myself said, 'How gladly I treat you like sons and give you a desirable land, the most beautiful inheritance of any nation.' I though you would call me Father' and not turn away from following me. - Jeremiah 3:19

Have we not all one Father? Did not one God create us?... - Malachi 2:10

Jesus said... *In the same way, let your light shine before men, that they may see your good deeds and praise your Father in heaven.* - Matthew 5:1

Jesus said... *Look at the birds of the air; they do not sow or reap or store away in barns, and yet your heavenly Father feeds them. Are you not much more valuable than they?* -Matthew 6:26

Jesus said... *No one knows the Son except the Father, and no one knows the Father except the son and those to whom the Son chooses to reveal him.* - Matthew 11:27

Scripture overload? Maybe. I encourage you to prayerfully read them again. God's Word is full of scriptures that point to His undying love for us. He created us with a purpose, one that He intends to see finish to a flourishing end. How can we know Jesus, and not know the Father? We can't; just as He said. However, we have to be willing to step before Him and ask for His provision, protection, and identity. We have to put our crowns on straight ladies and seek Him. Jesus stands at the door waiting to introduce us.

When I was in college, I wasn't in church. I lived away from home for a bit and never plugged into a church local to me. However, one night I had a dream that I remember so vividly. I recall being in a room so very bright it wasn't even white, it was brighter than white. My eyes couldn't see but when I tried to look up, I saw the hands and feet of Jesus. It was assurance that Jesus was there, right in the throne room, waiting on me. It's been nearly 20 years since that night and I remember it like it was yesterday. No, I couldn't see the Father, but I sensed His presence. I knew He was greater in that room and I knew that He was waiting on me.

For if you forgive men when they sin against you, your Heavenly Father will also forgive you. - Matthew 6:14

Sometimes it's difficult to believe God's truth. They seem so out of reach, like the one above. When I began praying for my marriage it became clear that my prayers for forgiveness were working to release healing in my marriage and relationship with my husband. I needed more forgiveness for my behavior than I needed to forgive my husband for his. I'm going to share with you an embarrassing moment that I'm ashamed of.

My husband worked 6 long, hard years for a company near us. He was never home, always tired, and I craved time with him. I resented the job but knew it was our provision. I would drive myself and our little boys up quite often to try to have lunch with him. He was always under pressure to perform and meet quotas. I only added to that pressure. One day, I picked him up for a lunch break, drove him to grab some fast food with plans to eat in his break room and on the way back with our lunch sacks and kids in the back an argument broke out. I cannot remember what the argument was over, clearly it wasn't that important. Anger rose up in me something fierce like it often did. My not so proudest moment in my marriage was when I reached into the sack as he was getting out of the car and threw his hamburger at him. It hit the ground and as I drove away I watched in my rear-view mirror as he knelt down and picked it up. He kneeled down and I'm sure he was furious. I'm sure he was upset about his lunch but mostly, I watched my husband break. He kneeled down to pick up scraps of food, all dignity lost, all honor gone, all the things I needed my husband to be, stripped away.

I had a decision to make as I drove my boys home. They were upset they didn't get to eat lunch with their Daddy, I was upset over words. Words. He's never called me names, he's never belittled me, he has never disrespected me with words. I was simply looking for any excuse to make him miserable, because I was miserable. It wasn't long after that, that I realized I had to do something different. I couldn't keep focusing on making him as miserable as myself. I had to start focusing on how I could be a better me, I was quite sick of the wife I had become. I didn't want to be known as the wife who threw hamburgers at her husband.

"...If God is for us, who can be against us?" - Romans 8:31

Can you think of a time when you dishonored your husband in such a way that it made him less of a man to the world? Maybe not. Maybe you've never done such a thing. However, it's more common than we'd like to admit. What I found is that I needed to forgive, to be forgiven, and to go back to God's plan for our marriage. Boy, did I have so much to learn.

He who did not spare his own Son but gave him up for us all - how will he not also, along with him, graciously give us all things. - Romans 8:32

That being forgiveness. That being the marriage He intended for us.

Approach the throne of Grace with confidence, so that we may receive mercy and find grace to help us in our time of need. - Hebrew 4:16

We can enter the throne room of God with no fear of punishment. We can enter His presence to ask for help. Most importantly, we can enter His presence to be reminded of who we are to Him, that includes our husbands. Who is your husband to God? Do you think that God sees the man your husband can be and expects you to help him become that great man of God in this broken world? Do you think that your role is of utmost important to God? He gave us the tools. He gave us His Son. He gave us a crown to remind us that we are His in a world that is looking for hope.

My marriage, ladies, is one that I am proud of. There are plenty of "hamburger moments" to be ashamed up but that's the beauty of what God can do. With His mercies that are new every day, we can leap up off of His mercy like a spring board every morning. We can throw on our armor and walk with Jesus straight to the Father. The door swings wide for His children. So, when I approach our Heavenly Father, I have found that He listens like I need a Daddy to listen. He loves like I need a Daddy to love. He provides like I need a Daddy to provide. He reminds me that He is my Daddy God.

He changes me little by little to become the mighty woman of God He needs me to be alongside the husband that He created me to lift up, honor, respect, and pray for. He does the same for each of us if we will just hold Jesus by the hand and enter the throne room.

Father, I come to you today to ask for forgiveness. I have sinned against my husband. I have dishonored the man You so carefully made and created. I have dishonored You in doing so. I need Your help, Daddy God. I am Your child and I have so much I need. You alone can meet every single one. Show me how I can be a better wife, show me how I can lift my husband up. Show me what honor for my husband can do for him and for our marriage. I thank you Lord for Your grace and mercy. Teach me, help me to be the wife you are calling me to be. Help me to see the little changes and blessings in my marriage as they move us closer to You. Give me a vision of our future together the way You see it. I desire to know Your heart. I claim the promises that You have given. I reject all lies that have been cast over our marriage like a net. Daddy God, I ask that you release our marriage from the expectations of the world where failure is common, and quitting is an option. In your Majesty, show me Your expectations and how majestic they are. Create in us a desire to know You first. Help my husband and I to walk in Your glory, hand in hand, to honor You. In Your Beloved Sons name, Amen.

DAY 34: THIRD PERSON

The Lord is still unraveling and unveiling so many things to me that I do not understand, things that have been taught to me during my 40 years that have been unclear are now coming into focus. The most important being, the Holy Spirit. My relationship with Jesus is beautiful and my growing relationship with the Father, understanding who He is to me, is being perfected. However, years back I felt a stirring in me that something was missing, and I honestly didn't know what.

But the Comforter, which is the Holy Ghost, whom the Father will send in My name, He shall teach you all the things, and bring all the things to your remembrance, whatsoever I have said unto you. - John 14:26 KJV

Likewise the Spirit helps us in our weakness. For we do not know what to pray for as we ought, but the Spirit Himself intercedes for us with groaning too deep for words - Romans 8:26

Out of all of the Trinity, the Person I understood the least was the Holy Spirit. I believe this may be the case for many Christians. His scriptural appearances vary greatly; a dove (Matt 3:16), a gust of wind (Acts 2:2), tongues of fire (Acts 2:3) and no one actually knows what the Spirit looks like. So, you can see why it has been hard for the last 40 years of my life to understand who He is.

He is a teacher, counselor, nurturer, and helper; to start with. Knowing this, you can see why it became very important for my marriage to better understand who this Person is I didn't know. He interacts in our lives and gifts of the Fruit of His Spirit. We only need to learn to follow His promptings and as our nurturer we can take our pain to Him.

And I will ask the Father, and he will give you another Counselor to be with you forever; the Spirit of truth. The world cannot accept him, because it neither sees him nor knows him. But you know him, for he lives with you and will be in you. - John 14:15 & 16

This scripture perfectly explains my struggle.

But when he, the Spirit of truth, comes, he will guide you into all truth. He will not speak on his own; he will speak only what he hears, and he will tell you what is yet to come. He will bring glory to me by taking from what is mine and making it known to you. - John 16:13 & 14

I grew up attending two churches, one a "Spirit Filled" church and the other a "Conservatively Spirit Filled". It was very confusing for me as a child, still saved by the grace of God and love of Jesus, but not understanding the third Person. It's all for His glory however.

A few years after my initial marriage study I was sitting in our new church home after a Sunday night sermon. I couldn't move. I felt paralyzed and kept saying to my husband "something is missing". It was so pressed upon me that I was missing something that I didn't want to leave until I had answers. Obviously, we couldn't stay all night and wait. On the drive home with so much passion in my heart I kept saying to my husband "I know I'm saved, I love my Jesus, but I feel like something is missing and I don't understand." He couldn't explain it, I couldn't explain it, but the Holy Spirit was trying to explain it.

I was simply missing a relationship with the Spirit. It's funny how God uses others influence to open your eyes, we are all just testimonies of His glory walking around, and the Spirit isn't going to be ignored. You love Jesus? You pray to the Father? Are you working on your relationship with the Spirit? I had no idea what that meant. A few days later I was laying across my bed praying about this feeling that would not settle. It was so deep within me. I looked up and saw a book on my husband's night stand called "Power". It was given to us by a friend whose church we attended a few months earlier. I sat up, opened it, and I read the words that went something like "Do you feel like something is missing?" Well! Yes, Lord I do!

For the next few hours I soaked up every word. Some of it was hard to swallow. Some of it was so brand new to me. I was hungry for it. I realized very quickly that I only needed to invite the Spirit to work in my life, He was waiting on me to submit and yield to Him.

Just this past year I attended two Bible conferences. One was the Women of Joy conference and it was amazing. I heard the Lord speak audibly to me in that small voice He uses and answered a prayer before I left that I consider a miracle. That's a story for another day. A week or so later I found myself at another conference called, Fire. I encountered the Holy Spirit like never before and what I walked away with was a relationship that I needed. I heard someone tell this story that another evangelical preacher had shared and I'm sorry to say I don't know his name. The story goes something like this...

When I go to large events to preach the sanctuary will fill with people. I am put into a room to wait. I stay there quietly wishing I could get out. I've been told to stay here and pray for those coming in to hear me preach but all I really want to do is go out and start praying over, loving, and speaking life into those coming in. I'm locked away in a tiny room when I could be working and moving among God's people. THAT, is exactly what we do to the Holy Spirit. We allow Him into us and we lock Him away. We say to Him, stay right here, pray for me and I'll come get you when I need you to do something big. Instead, what He wants to do is walk with you through your every move, your every moment, your every word in the world and guide you, pray with you, teach you, share God's love. Still, He waits and prays, and we feel His presence, we know He is there.

Sister, are you feeling this? If you want to see miracles in your marriage you have to release the Spirit in your life. You have to put on your armor, pick up your tools, and tell Him to show out! The gracious thing that the Spirit does for us is not overpower us, He waits for us to give Him permission to be the Power! Can you imagine what that power will do?

There is a song we sing in church regularly by Jeremy Camp and every time my hands fly up in praise because I know what it means. My desire is to help others understand what I am learning. The song goes.

The same power that rose Jesus from the grave

The same power that commands the dead to wake

Lives in us, lives in us

The same power that moves mountains when He speaks

The same power that can calm a raging sea

Lives in us, lives in us

He lives in us, lives in us

Ladies, this power is for us. It's in us. Believe!

Are you committed to making your marriage stronger? Are you ready for the power that Jesus sent to us to take over in your marriage?

You may not believe it now, you may not see it now, it may not yet be truth but sister, your husband is being called to be a great man of God.

It took a stranger praying over me during the Fire conference for my eyes to be opened to fact. My husband was not raised in church but had a daddy that love the Lord. His daddy prayed for his children and wife. Tragically, he was taken at a very young age, when his babies were little. He was a great man of God, everyone says so that knew him. When I met my husband when we were 12 years old, he did not know if he believed in God. He was not in church growing up. When we started dating at the tender age of 14, and our parents were driving us to the movies, he still did not believe. Sister, I believed enough for him to catch it. I told my future husband that I had to introduce him to the Savior that loved him more than I did. It didn't take long before Jesus captured his heart and he had much to learn. We've been together almost 26 years and we are both still learning.

Are you praying for your husband to become a great man of God? Do you see him as that? Do you see past his mistakes or do you see his future self? When Jesus talks about the miracles that happen when we "just believe", He is speaking truth. It's time to let go of all you think you know, and embrace the truth, surrender your life, your marriage in whole (not in part) to Him.

Pray with me.

Lord Father, I want to thank you for all Your grace, all Your mercy, and all Your blessings. Lord, thank You for pressing into me the things You need me to know. I understand that there is so much I may never know until I reach Your presence in Glory, and that there are mysteries you are looking to reveal to me here. I want to receive them all, Father. Thank you, Jesus, for making a way and being a friend to me during my troubled times and celebrating with me during this life journey. Now, Spirit, I need You. I need You to show up in my life and show out. Teach me about the power of You that resides in Me. Show me how I can pray for my husband and our marriage. Spirit, bring me comfort and wisdom during the hard times. I know that the evil one is lurking to steal, kill, and destroy what God sees as good. My marriage is a good thing, help me to be the wife that sees my husband as You see him. Lord, thank You for Your patience, protection, and truth. In the name of Jesus, my sweet Savior. Amen

.

DAY 35: DELAY TO DEVELOP

before any plant of the field was in the earth and before any herb of the field had grown. For the Lord God had not caused it to rain on the earth, and there was no man to till the ground; - Genesis 2:5

There was a time on this earth when it was completely barren of a garden. It was a just a hot, humid dust ball where nothing flourished because there was nothing to flourish.

There was a day just before the planting.

The earth was not capable of bringing forth its own fruit, it was not able to plant itself. Plus, two factors were missing to cause a garden to flourish, rain and someone to tend it.

Do you ever feel like your marriage is going through a dry spell; no refreshing rain, no tending? Have you ever heard the saying "You may think the grass is greener on the other side, but if you take the time to water your own grass, it would be just as green?" Are you looking at your dry side and peering over to the other side wishing your grass was green and lush again? I can't imagine any marriage that does not experience this. Be patient; water and tend a little to what you've been given.

When the earth was so hot that water existed only in the form of vapor, there could be no vegetation. Rain began to pour, the vapor condensed to form the seas and the vegetation, planted by God, began to clothe the cool ground of the earth. A garden was in the making. It required His planting; the earth could not do it on its own.

A garden was rising up out of what was once the dry dust. Its vegetation started reaching towards the heavens and became fruitful. This narrative in

God's Word was not just a description of the beginning of our world, but of man's relationship to God and in turn, our relationship with our husbands.

I want to talk about this dry time in your marriage because it's important to recognize it for what it is. During this time when things are very uncomfortable, when we begin looking for a sign that there is grass greener elsewhere; it's time to ask God for reassurance concerning your own grass. God created the heavens, the moon, the stars, and all the things we marvel. Even after all that beauty in the beginning there was a moment when, the earth seemed hopeless. Your marriage will mimic God's perfect plan. You fell in love, everything was wonderful and then you start waiting for the garden. We all know what happens next...

God's power!

Jehovah himself planted the seeds into the darkness of the earth and that seed held within itself, the miracle of another seed. There may be a time in your marriage when there seems to be no fruit, when there seems to be no refreshing rain, when there seems to be no one tending to the planting of the garden that will ultimately produce the fruit we long for.

I am here to tell you, sister, that you just pray and wait. The rain is coming, and the seeds are being planted. The garden is about to rise up. God is not withholding from you the marriage you desire. That is a lie of Satan that was told from the very beginning. God is not withholding. He is simply preparing. I like to call this time a "Delay to Develop". It feels like withholding and we've probably heard it a million times "God is withholding a blessing because you need to..." Nope. Ladies, that is a lie. There is a delay because the miracle is unfolding where you cannot see it. The rain is coming, the earth will be quenched, and the seeds will produce fruit.

God's timing is sometimes forgotten in this day and age. We live in a time when we want results, and we want them now. We pray and want to open our eyes and see a miracle. The greatest miracles I have ever experienced in my life were those that I did not know He had coming. I may have given up hope and questioned His will. Then He says, "It's not yours, it's Mine." Isn't it all His? What feels like a withholding in your marriage is actually, God's great love. The disappointments we feel in the wait are His greatest acts of love. We find freedom when we remove the restrictions we have placed on Him and surrender. If you don't believe me...ask Him.

Accepting, knowing, and trusting that even the delays in our marriage, life, and prayers is stepping into hope. When you can strip away your disappointments with God your view of the otherwise changes. You become excited about what He is planting for you. You are encouraged knowing that something beautiful is about to spring up, you appreciate the tenderness that rises out of the darkness and grows so big and strong that in and of itself produces the fruit you need over and over. The miracles are planted and there are miracles within those miracles.

Even in God's Word the garden that He so perfectly planted in the beginning, that was so craved and longed for ultimately is berated by sin. God will plant that perfect garden, because truly your marriage is His, not yours. He will put you on the perfect path surrounded by all of His miracles. The human part of us, the flesh, even after the garden, will wander off the path and into the thorns from time to time. We may forget that He needs us to tend to things, we forget to ask for His help, we try to do it all on our own and we will find that we need His restoration in our marriage. The beauty of it all, is that the garden of this life's journey is nothing compared to the one He has waiting for us in glory. Trust that your marriage, when in a dry spell, is about to unfold many miracles.

Lord Father, I thank You today for your unseen miracles. I thank You for Your perfect timing. I thank You for the dry spells because they too serve a purpose. I thank You for the grass that is greener because it gives me hope. Lord, you are my Lord and I trust Your perfect plan for my marriage. Help my faith when it is small. Help my unbelief when I don't see the miracles. When my marriage feels dry and barren, remind me Lord of Your planting. Thank you, Jesus, for your great love and redemption. Spirit teach me and nurture my marriage. I come to You. Oh God, asking for your blessings in my life. Send the rain, Lord. In Jesus name, Amen

DAY 36: CHILDLIKE

And said, "Truly, I say to you, unless you turn and become like children, you will never enter the kingdom of heaven. - Matthew 18:3

Truly, I say to you, whoever does not receive the kingdom of God like a child shall not enter. - Luke 18:17

Whoever humbles himself like this child is the greatest in the kingdom of heaven. -Matthew 18:4

What is Jesus telling us to do in the above text? Regarding your relationship with God what would this look like? Regarding your relationship to your husband, what would this look like?

One of my favorite things to witness is a couple who has been together for many years enjoying each other's company like children do. When I'm in a restaurant I always notice when there is an older couple and I can tell right away if they have a playful relationship. It always does my heart good to see them still enjoying each other's company as if they are young again and still in love.

What are some positive changes that have taken place in you since your relationship with your husband began? What about your husband, what positive changes has he made? Have you ever tried to change something about each other? How did that work?

One of first things God pressed on me when we were struggling in our marriage was that I could no longer focus on my husband and how he needed to change? I needed to focus on myself and get out of God's way. If God needed my husband to change in anyway, He was in charge of making that happen. I was not. I needed to move myself out of the way and learn to be softer and quieter, more childlike in my approach to him. Not to lower myself, but so that God could be heard over me. I was the voice in my husband's ear far too many times when God was trying to be the voice.

I needed to learn to have that childlike faith in the Father. I needed to learn to be humble and trusting. I needed to get myself out of the way and focus on my relationship with God first. I humbled myself like a child and handed my husband over as well. If I wanted to see a real change in our relationship, I had to trust that God would do right by us both.

My fondest memories of my husband are when he does act like a child. I don't mean he thinks like a child and makes decisions like a child. I mean he loves me with a pure love that is free. When he scoops me up in his arms, knowing I'll wiggle a little because my love language isn't touch and his is. He holds on tight and while it makes me a bit uncomfortable, it's when I give in that he's at his sweetest. Just the other day he was aggravating me, and I pretended to karate chop at him. He wrapped his arms tight around me and I put my hand up like a blade to his neck and said, 'watch out, I've got a mean throat punch" and as my hand touched his neck he laughed and said, "that tickles, if that is what your throat punches feel like you can do it more often." I think he sounded like a 7-year-old, but I got tickled at his playfulness. Sometimes, we just need to be like little children with each other, pretending or playing in such a fashion that it makes the stress of the world disappear. My favorite thing to do is to make him laugh, I don't know why he thinks I'm so funny but sometimes he just laughs. Those moments are the ones that mean the most to us.

The Lord has been speaking to me a great deal lately on being more childlike in my relationships with my husband and my children. It's hard to be childlike with my kids and be the adult in charge because I am their parent, I handle their lives as if they are the most important thing in the world, but nothing matters more to my children than the moments when I get down on their level and play. I get to know them best on their level of play and thinking. They get to see the child in me that is still there. With all that, their respect grows for me because they know I care about them on a level that is deeper than just being "mom". The same goes for my husband. Inside of him is that little boy who didn't have it so easy growing up. Inside of my husband, that big man, that great man of God, is a boy who loved his big wheel, cherished his hot wheels, loved to fish, and loved to explore nature. Inside of me is that little girl who loved her dolls, loved to climb trees and build things, loved to pretend and play. Sometimes those children just need to play together.

Inside you and your husband, there is the same. I would be willing to bet that guards would come down, stress levels would decrease, and tension would melt away if we could all, for a moment, be like little children. As wives, we can humble ourselves and let God work on our husbands. In the meantime, we need to be His child. We need to let Him love us, and us Him the way children should love and be loved. We need to trust and have faith in such a pure way that we can see only the love our Father has for us. He loves our husbands the same way. Pray with me.

Daddy God, thank you. Thank You for loving us the way a Father is supposed to love. Thank You for loving us so much that You created us to be loved. My husband and I are both Your children. Lord, show us and teach us what it means to be children in Your kingdom. Show us how to do Your work here in this life journey as adults but also to love each other with such a pure love. Show us how to enjoy each other's company and spirits. Give us wisdom to understand the child that is inside each of us. Help us to approach each other with the kind of love that mimics Your own for us. Helps us to be forgiving and understand. Help us to be resilient when we are hurt. Help us to give each other the kind of love that we both deserve to experience in this life together. Jesus thank you for being our friend and showing us how important our relationship is in the Kingdom work here. We know that we cannot save the marriages of others, but we certainly can be an example of what is possible when a couple clings to you like children cling to their Father or Mother. Spirit impart on us wisdom and grace, give us discernment for each other's needs. Thank you for all that you have provided. I claim your healing power over my marriage today. In Jesus Mighty name, Amen.

DAY 37: CARRYING BAGGAGE

Is this not the fast that I have chosen: to loose the bonds of wickedness, to undo the heavy burdens, toilet the oppressed go free, and that you break every yoke? - Isaiah 58:6

Cast all your burden on the Lord, and He shall sustain you; He shall never permit the righteous to be moved. - Psalm 55:22

Come to Me, all you who labor and are heavy laden, and I will give you rest. Take My yoke upon you and learn from Me, for I am gentle and lowly in heart, and you will find rest for your souls. For My yoke is easy and My burden is light. - Matthew 11:28-30

For I, the Lord your God, will hold your right hand, saying to you, "Fear not, I will help you" - Isaiah 41:13

Sisters, I believe with all my heart that this is a topic I could dedicate an entire book to. As women, we LOVE to pick up others burdens and carry them around. Scripture does call us to help others with their burdens (Galatians 6:2). However, as believers in Christ, we are instructed to hand Him whatever it is that is weighing us down.

We when enter marriage with another, we are joined together with each other's past. Someone once told me I was lucky to have been with my husband since we were young, that we did not bring anything into our marriage from other relationships. I'm here to tell you, that may or may not be true, we still had baggage. The scares of life shape us and make us who we are and the experiences that cause those scares, the people that may have inflicted the brokenness, can come into the relationship as baggage. Past heart breaks, broken dreams, death, loss, the stripping away of innocence too soon, the relationships that were broken, and so much more; they all are compartmentalized in our brains and we carry them with us. It doesn't matter where you've been or what you've walked through, you have something you are carrying, and its heaviness isn't even meant for you to carry.

We all go through life carrying these things. We can't seem to let them go. Sometimes, we pick up the baggage that our spouse brings, and we carry that too. It may not seem like such a big deal at first, I mean, we are called to share in each other's burdens and help each other. However, at some point, God is going to call you into "deep waters". There's going to be a journey He needs you to take together in this life. It's going to be scary and hard.

I keep going back to the image of the lonely boat out over the water, the waves crashing with the wind, and Jesus walking towards the boat. (Matthew 14:22-33) Jesus told his followers to get in a boat and go on ahead. He stayed behind and prayed. Before day break Jesus walked out to them and they were afraid. Jesus told them not be afraid and Peter was the brave one who would step out of the boat. At the sound of Jesus' voice, he stepped out, fully trusting, but the wind...the wind scared him, and he sank. Yes, Jesus saved him upon Peter's call.

Here's the thing. Sometimes Jesus calls us out into the deep. He expects us to walk with Him without fear. Do you want to step out carrying that baggage you've had with you all this time? I'll tell you right now, I did exactly that. I had stood on the shore for years wondering what it would be like to be in those deep waters with Jesus and when I was called out I had so much baggage weighing me down. The deep waters are where you'll find Jesus and it's the best and safest place to be, with Him.

There used to be a time when I had never heard the Lord speak to me. This might be your situation too. I promise, He is trying to help you hear Him. One day during a praise moment between God and myself I felt in my spirit Him telling me "*you carried the baggage into deep waters that I never intended you to carry, as soon as you let go, you will float to the top and walk on water with me.*"

That moment will forever be burned into my soul. I may still, from time to time, pick up baggage but I have learned to hand it over to Christ. He expects us to hand it over to Him. Give it to him.

You know you're carrying something, you may be ready to give it over or you may be in denial. Here is what I want you to do.

Pray.

You don't want to get out in those deep waters until you've given your baggage over. If you're in the deep waters...let go immediately. Get with Jesus and ask Him to show you what baggage you're are carrying. Ask Him to show you just how heavy it is and then ask Him to take it. Start handing it to Him piece by piece as quickly as you can. Be free of the weight of the past, your past or your husbands. Your freedom to move forward in this life with Christ is waiting.

I knew what I had been carrying. I knew the feelings I associated with what was inside my baggage AND the feelings I had as a result of how heavy they were. Imagine being released of all of that. It is not yours to carry. It's not! I could go on and on with scripture and here are a few more.

Therefore humble yourselves under the mighty hand of God, that He may exalt you in due time, casting all your care upon Him, for He cares for you. - 1 Peter 5:6,7

Even to your old age, I am He, and even to gray hairs I will carry you. I have made, and I will bear; even I will carry, and will deliver you. -Isaiah 46:6

The righteous cry out, and the Lord hears, and delivers them out of all their troubles. - Psalm34:17

No matter what baggage you are carrying around that is affecting your marriage, cast it on Jesus. Give it to Him. Ask Him to help you. I personally, have to ask Jesus to take it from me. Sometimes giving it isn't something I'm able to do because my grip is so tight, and I promise, even asking Him to take it, He snatches it right up and it's gone. Free!

Jesus, oh how I thank You for all You offer to do for me. You have saved me and covered all my sin and all my shame. Nothing I could do in this life would have ever been enough. I thank You now for being who You are at all times. Remove from me the heavy weight, the burdens, the baggage, the things of this life that I have carried for far too long. Free me Jesus! Lord thank You for Your mercies. Thank You for providing a Way. I do not want to go through this life drowning in deep waters, I do not want to go through this life standing safely on the water's edge either. I want to walk on water with you Jesus. I want to hold Your hand and know that I have been set free. Father God, bless my marriage through this. Make our marriage one that You can use as an example to others of what You have in store. This life is short, and our time here is unknown. Spirit give me the wisdom to know when I have picked up something I should not be carrying and give it straight to You, help me to NOT cast those burdens onto others through actions or words. Help me to simply give them to you. Teach me how to give the burdens others have shared with me to You. Help me to show others that the can do the same. Help me to show my husband that it is possible. In Jesus Mighty name I pray, Amen.

DAY 38: HIS LOVE

I slept but my heart was awake.
Listen! My lover is knocking:
"Open to me, my sister, my darling,
my dove, my flawless one.
My head is drenched with dew,
my hair with dampness of the night".
- Song of Songs 5:2

When the Lord first gave me this scripture I admit I was completely confused by it but not surprised. I knew He would have much to teach me here and boy did He. Praying for wisdom before starting a new day of study always leads to a deeper lesson for me and I pray that as you read this, you see the importance of this scripture as well and at the end of today's devotion, come back and read it again through the eyes that Christ has opened for you.

I had to back up and read a little more of the verses surrounding the scripture to begin my understanding of it so let me explain to you what I learned. This is "The Bride" telling another distressing dream. Have you ever dreamed of losing something you loved? I have had horrible dreams of losing my husband or even my children through years. It's very distressing. So, the bride here is telling of a dream. I put "The Bride" in quotations because as we know, "The Bride" is also the church of Christ. Jesus is about to show us once again how our marriage mimics the Gospel and the relationship that God desires with us. I am going to scripture dump on you because the Word is where our wisdom is found. Hang with me because it took me a bit to understand where this little journey would take me as well.

Let's start with the work of the "Bridegroom", Jesus...

So, they went away by themselves in a boat to a solitary place. But many who saw them leaving recognized them and ran on foot from the towns and got there ahead of them. When Jesus landed and saw a large group, he had compassion on them, because they were like sheep without a shepherd. So, he began teaching them many things. -Mark 6:32-34

Jesus went through all the towns and villages, teaching in their synagogues, preaching the good news of the kingdom and healing every disease and sickness. When he saw the crowds, he had compassion on them, because they were harassed and helpless, like sheep without a shepherd. ^- Matthew 9:35-36

One of those days Jesus went out to a mountainside to pray and spend the night praying to God. - Luke 6:12

In the words of Jesus: *The servant came back and reported this to his master. Then the owner of the house became angry and ordered his servant, 'Go out quickly into the streets and alleys of the town and bring in the poor, the crippled, the blind, and the lame.' 'Sir," the servant said, 'what you ordered had been done, but there is still room.' "Then the master told his servant, 'Go out to the roads and country lanes and make them come in, so that my house will be full.'"* - Luke 14:21-23

Let's read the Songs verse above again.

What we don't see is that the bride in Songs is satisfied with her washed feet, clean and ready for bed, while the bridegroom, his "head drenched with dew" and "hair with the dampness of the night", is toiling for others, working. He has worked hard and is ready for his bride to let him in. The state of the bride is not one of sin but one of neglect of service. "The Bride" doesn't want to get her feet dirty and answer the door, later she finds, when she finally does answer, that her Lover has moved on and she is such distress because she cannot find Him, she is lost and the world attacks her, she realizes all she ever wanted was right there begging for her.

Ladies, the Lover of our Soul is knocking on our door and He has worked so hard, day and into the night, sharing the Gospel so that no one is left, that everyone is invited in.

Let's talk about how this applies to our hearts and our marriage.

From day one of this marriage study I have kept the focus on how God's Word can help you become a better wife. I put absolutely no focus whatsoever on how you can make your husband a better husband other than through the power of prayer and despite what many of us believe about our husbands, believe now that Jesus believes your husband is a great man of God. Jesus himself will toil and work, the Spirit will intercede when you do not, to win your husbands heart to the Him. Always remember the world is ready for an attack. I have many conversations, so many, with women who say they want their husbands to pray more, to tithe, to go to church, to seek a relationship with Christ, to be saved, and the list goes on and on. I hear you, my heart always wants my husband to grow in Christ too, and I prayed all those things for him as well. First, we must begin praying for that relationship with Christ to grow; for ourselves and for our husbands. Don't be discouraged because it is your diligence in prayer that will make a difference.

Again, so many scriptures were given to me for this day's devotion. If you don't have your Bible out or your Bible App open, get ready because here they come, and I want you to put the work in here of looking them up.

Matthew 28:18-19 = All authority
Proverbs 1: 20-23 = Wisdom is calling, respond.
Acts 13:46 = Don't reject Him.
1 Samuel 2:8 = He raises the poor up and gives them an inheritance.
James 2:5 = The poor in the eye of the world are rich in faith.
2 Peter 3:9 = He is patient for your salvation.
2 Corinthians 5:20 = WE ARE AMBASSADORS

We are ambassadors for Christ's love. In order to understand the love Christ has for us, we need to focus on our love affair with Him. How can we love a lost and dying world, how can we love our lost husbands, how can we fully love if we don't first love Jesus? We can't. It's time ladies that we recognize that Jesus has already done all we need Him to do and we just need to put ourselves in the vulnerable place of letting Him love us deeply, He can meet that love need we have so that we can focus on our husbands and marriage in prayer.

He has such great things in store for us and our marriage. A heavenly inheritance awaits. Stay the course, stay in prayer.

All scripture points to the Gospel. So, with that in mind, we can approach all scripture as if it's the Good News. As you pray for your marriage and husband today, remember that the "Bride" and even ourselves as wives may be neglecting what we are called to do because we don't want to get our feet dirty. Is it possible that we have found a comfy place and have prepared ourselves for our own rest when Jesus is knocking and asking us to be His hands and feet? If you have given up on your marriage or your husband, is it now time to rise up. Are you satisfied, while He is not?

Enter the Throne Room of God by locking arms with Jesus. Dance before the Lord with joy for what He is about to do just because of you coming to Him and asking Him all those questions that you have concerning your marriage and your husband. Ask that He rain down His blessings on your marriage and show your husband favor. Let Him show you what is possible. Pray with me.

God Father, all of heaven roars Your name. You are Mighty and how excellent is Your name in all the earth. You set Your glory above the heavens and the earth. When I think that you have orchestrated my marriage as perfectly as you orchestrated the sun and moon and stars, no praise is high enough for how great You are. I thank You for all the blessings You are about to rain down in my marriage. Lord, what a mighty God we serve that the angels bow before You and You are willing to show my husband favor. Remind me that I am a good thing. I adore You God and I am ready to serve You. Show me Lord how I can be Your hands and feet in my marriage and for my husband so that the world can see what is possible. Work Your miracles in my marriage Lord just as Jesus did for the broken and hurting here on earth. All glory, all honor, all praise is to You Lord for you are so mighty in Your ways. Hallelujah, in Jesus Holy name, Amen.

DAY 39: SO THAT

God of hope, fill me with all joy and peace as I trust in You, so that I may overflow with hope by the power of the Holy Spirit. - Romans 15:13

Oh, how many times I have gone to my Father in prayer for another's marriage. How many times I have I watched a marriage fall completely apart. How many times I have questioned as to why this happens and why can't "I" help. Then the Lord softly spoke to me concerning this heavy weight of my heart "I don't expect you to fix their marriage. I expect you to show them what is possible." When I heard in my Spirit these words whispered so gently and unexpectedly I knew that I could hand over all of that heavy weight I had carried to Him. He is going to show you what is possible, what you choose to do with that is up to you.

You're hope for your marriage is not found in this study. It is found in the power of the Holy Spirit.

You have come 39 out of 40 days with me. You have journeyed through God's Word and He still has more for us. As you yield, the Holy Spirit will share these blessing with you and you can believe that they are coming.

Be joyful in hope, patient in affliction, faithful in prayer. - Romans 12:12

1 Th 5:17 simply tells us that we are to pray continually, and it is of utmost importance that you are faithful with your prayer. Your prayer will unlock the blessings that are waiting to cascade from heaven down on your marriage. Be patient, they are coming as you are faithful, and you can find so much joy in that promise, in that hope.

The mind of a sinful man is death, but a mind controlled by the Spirit is life and peace. - Romans 8:6

I'm treading as lightly as I can here, but this must be said, and toes will get stepped on. I make no apologies. I experience such negativity and words from wives as they speak "death" over their marriage. They wait until the divorce papers arrive or their husbands to walk out and then I get the email,

I get the Facebook message, or I get a text that says, "pray for me, my husband just left", "pray for me, my marriage is over", "pray for me, my husband doesn't love me, and he walked out." Ladies, this is speaking death over your marriage before you've even begun to believe that God has something different for you. I'll address this lack of faith in a bit. If you are speaking death and not life over your marriage, not matter how "dead" you believe it is, then stop now. STOP NOW. Jesus raised humans, with hearts that no longer had a beat, from the dead. He surely can raise a seemingly dead marriage. As the scripture above says "a mind controlled by the Spirit is life and peace". Speak LIFE! With the power of the Holy Spirit, start telling your giant just how big your God is. Have faith and when you don't have faith, ask for it.

Faith and trust in your God is imperative towards moving forward in your marriage with strength and belief, with joy and hope.

...but now revealed and made known through the prophetic writings by the command of the eternal God, so that all nations might believe and obey him - Romans 16:26

The weight of that scripture is not lost on me. Is it lost on you? The promises of God that were commanded by God to be written for you today so that you might believe and obey him are powerful and real. Your belief level should have just risen 100% straight to the top. Believe and obey.

Adam's belief in God's promises were so big! So, big in fact, that he named his wife based on the promises that God gave. We are coming full circle today from the model of marriage in the beginning of this study to the belief of LIFE through faith here at the end.

Adam named his wife Eve, because she WOULD become the mother of all living. - Genesis 3:20 (emphasis added)

The essence of faith consists in believing and receiving what God has revealed. Consider what God has revealed to you over the last 39 days. Then the Lord showed me this.

These were all commended for their faith, yet none of them received what had been promised. - Hebrews 11:39

When the Lord first directed me to the above scripture I was without a doubt confused. The preceding scriptures went on and on about the heroes of faith and how the world was not worthy of them. Yet, none of them had received what had been promised. The reality is, faith enables us to turn from the approval of the world and seek only the approval of God. If God is glorified by delivering His people, He will do it. If He sees fit to be glorified by not delivering His people, then He will do that. But we must NEVER believe that the absence for deliverance means a lack of faith. That was why He showed me this scripture. To teach me about His ways and not my own. To teach me about faith and trust. God sees the faithful and the faithful see Him.

All these people were still living by faith when they died. They did not receive the things promised; they only saw them and welcomed them from a distance. - Hebrews 11:13

Lord, increase our faith.

Increase our faith...

...*so that*, for our salvation, we may have a personal trust in You, apart from excellent and praiseworthy works, as we are delivered from our sins and raised again because of our justification. (Ro. 4:5, 23-25, 5:1)

so that in prayer, faith is the "confidence we have in approaching God: that if we ask anything according to His will, he hears us." (1Jn 5:14)

so that when we reference the things unseen of which Scripture speaks, faith will give us substance to them, so that we act upon the condition of their reality, (Heb. 11:1-3)

and *so that* faith is a working principal in our life, and we are able to use faith as illustrated in Your Word.

Faith looks to the future. That is where the greatest rewards are found.

Without faith it is impossible to please God - Hebrews 11:6

This kind of faith grows as we study on His Word and participate in worship and prayer. Faith is possible to all kinds of believers in all kinds of situations. It is a necessity for all of God's people.

God has planned something better for us so that only together with us would they be made perfect. -Hebrews 11:40

What a beautiful ending to a chapter.

Father God, increase my Faith. When my faith feels so small, help me to trust in You completely. Help me to speak life over my marriage with the strength and gentleness of the Holy Spirit. Give me an eternal perspective of what is possible in my marriage and help me see beyond my present circumstances. God of hope, fill me with all joy and peace as I trust in You, so that I may overflow with hope by the power of the Holy Spirit. Help me to be joyful in hope, patient in affliction, and faithful in prayer. Lord, I want to live as a wife that pleases You. I know that I must have faith in Your dreams and plans for my marriage despite what the world tells me. Lord, thank you for all the goodness You have waiting and see us through the battles and storms that rage. When the world tries to rip us a part, show us how to cling to one another by clinging to You. Holy Spirit teach me to speak life over my husband, our marriage, and our future. No longer will I allow my tongue to speak death. Jesus thank You for Your sacrifice so that I may forever have faith in Your love for us. In the precious name of Jesus, I pray, Amen.

t

DAY 40: DON'T GIVE UP

Father, thank You for helping me to understand that the access I have gained into Your grace in which I now stand has come to me by faith. Help me to rejoice in the hope of Your glory! -Romans 5:2

Imagine trying to wrap up 40 days of a marriage study. I wanted it to go out with a bit of a bang, a powerful Word and I knew there was no way I could do it on my own. So, after much prayer before opening God's Word for this last day, I opened my Bible.

Galatians.

At the time that Paul was writing, the Galatian churches were facing a double threat. One involved the purity of the doctrine and the other involved the purity of conduct. Certain individuals had come into the area who would "pervert the Gospel of Christ" (Gal 1:7, 5:10) They insisted that while salvation was of Jesus Christ, works were also necessary for salvation. In the book of Galatians Paul destroys all arguments in favor of mixing law with faith. Paul answers this argument by declaring the truth of the sanctifying power of the Holy Spirit, and the richness of life available when He rules the Christian with whom He indwells.

I believe the reason that this Book was deemed so important for the last day of this study is because the world is about to start telling you that your "works alone" as a wife are what will save your marriage and He wants the glory of saving it for you. No matter what your marriage looks like at this very moment, He wants to be the One that abides within it. Boy, that sure takes the pressure off of us. We don't have to worry about how we "perform" as wives as long as we are trusting in Him.

Paul was hot mad when he began writing the letter to the Galatians. He opened his letter with love but dove right into what was making him angry. The world was seeping into what needed to stay pure. Faith in what Christ had done for the world would bring about salvation for the world and that was being perverted by the world.

You have come so far by completing these 40 days of studying on your role in your marriage and through prayer that it is imperative that you not let the world influence your behavior at the close of this day. You are to still continue to spend time in prayer, seek guidance from the Spirit, and have faith at all times that your marriage matters to God.

Be diligent in trying not to win the approval of the world, but of God. If you are trying to please the world, you are not a servant of Christ. Remember, sisters, that the gospel that we believe is not something that man or the world made up, it was received by revelations from Jesus Christ. The life that we live is the result of Christ living in us. Our lives are a reflection for Christ and not of the world. We died to our self with Christ so that we can live by faith in Him who loves us and gave himself for us.

As we move forward from today, we must continue in prayer for our marriage and our husbands. You are running a good race. Don't let the world confuse you and always remember who the author of confusion is, go back to Scripture when you are unsure. Go back to prayer when you need wisdom. Trust the Spirit that gives us victory over sin for the sinful nature desires what is opposite of the Spirit. Sin and the Spirit are always in conflict against one another so that you do not do what you want but what the Spirit want, let the Spirit lead.

But the fruit of the Spirit is love, joy, peace, patience, kindness, goodness, faithfulness, gentleness, and self-control. Against such things there is no law - Galatians 5:22-23

When the world is telling you to be the opposite of these things towards your husband or others, it's time to take a step back. It's time to get back into God's Word and seek His Throne room, where you belong. When your husband is opposite of those things and "caught in sin, you who are spiritual should restore him gently." (Gal 6:1)

We have a responsibility that is greater than our own desires. We are being called to operate in our new life, as new creations, as something beautiful and pure. Just a few days ago the Bride of Christ as referred to as a "dove, my flawless one" (Songs 5:2, 6:7) Christ sees you through a different lens than the world does. We should also strive to see our husbands through the same lens of Christ. Do not become weary in doing good, for at the proper time we will reap a harvest if we do not give up. (Galatians 6:9)

I would like to leave you with this. Years ago, I sat down with my heart and my Bible open and let God pour His love and wisdom into me concerning my marriage.

Sometimes, I read what I have written and step back and say, "Did I write that?" It's because the mind forgets but it is all planted deeply within me. His Word and my faith in Him changed my marriage. It is different. Our marriage is good. We have had some major battles since I completed this study the first time, some likely would have ripped our marriage to shreds. The devil has tried to chew us up and spit us out. Prayer is what got us through it. Even in our darkest moments, we started seeking light and we always found it in Christ.

I love to ask people I meet how long they have been married, sometimes the numbers astound me. I then like to ask what their secret is, and the answer is almost universally, **"we never gave up."**

Father God, the world will come at us like a freight train. My husband and I will, from time to time, feel like our marriage has taken a beating. We will feel like our marriage is being chewed up and spit out by the world. Father, I ask you today to put a hedge of protection around our marriage, guard our hearts, and send your angels armies out to protect what you have put together so perfectly. Help us to always seek you first when there is a giant standing in front of us or a mountain we must climb. Lord, we trust you. We have faith in you. We look forward to the joy that will spill out and over flow on the world through this gift, this marriage, you have given us. Thank You Jesus for your love and sacrifice as the example of how we should love. Spirit continue to lead, guide, and direct us as we move about this world. Help us to discern what is not of You. Lord, again we thank You for all your blessings, gifts, and favor. Give us the strength and wisdom to never give up. In Jesus name we pray, Amen.

ABOUT THE AUTHOR

AIMEE LARSEN is a Christian wife, mother, entrepreneur, teacher, writer, speaker, and philanthropist. A country girl at heart, she grew up next door to the family farm in Northwest Georgia. She married her high school sweet heart, James, and they have built their home and family together for the last 17 years. As a mother of five and family personally touched by foster care and adoption, Aimee strives to be the voice for all families and children, while sharing the hope of Christ. The founder of Flourish Foster Care Closet & Support, she has spent countless hours helping to provide the foster care communities of North Georgia with clothing and much needed support. Her dream of writing to strengthen the family unit is punctuated by her education and background in child development, early childhood education, and as a specialist in reading diagnostics. Aimee is a two time graduate of Berry College in Mt. Berry, GA. Author of Homespun Mom & Homespun Threads, Aimee has spent years writing and sharing with other women about her faith, creativity, and passion for family.

Connect with Aimee and learn more about her ministry at www.aimeelarsen.com

"And He said to them, 'Go into all the world and preach the gospel to every creature." -Mark 16:15 NKJV

www.ingramcontent.com/pod-product-compliance
Lightning Source LLC
LaVergne TN
LVHW012104160826
845678LV00014B/2923

* 9 7 8 1 7 2 1 8 3 4 6 2 4 *